What people are saying about

Modron: Meeting the Celtic Mother G

Modron is a Goddess whom, for
has scarcely been given the attention she deserves among Celtic polytheists today. Perhaps one reason for this is because she is somewhat elusive. In this book, BanDea takes us on a journey to meet the Mother Goddess. Uncovering her lore, her worship, and her splendour. From the stories of the Mabinogi, to her connection with wells and water, and even with the Otherworld, this book offers a leaping board for any who hear the call of Modron. More than just a textbook on Modron's legend and lore, this book also offers insights on how to develop a working relationship with this Goddess, written by someone who quite clearly holds a deep, passionate, and profound reverence for Her. A deeply personal and thoughtful book indeed.
Mhara Starling, author of *Welsh Witchcraft*

What a fascinating and mysterious deity; the author has shone a light into the world of Modron in this wonderful book. From her myths and legends, to working with her in modern times, this book is a real treasure.
Rachel Patterson, author of over 25 books on witchcraft including *The Cailleach* and *Gods and Goddesses of England*

Modron explores everything we know or can suppose about this enigmatic and obscure goddess, creating a fuller picture of who she was and is. This short introductory text also offers vital insight and context into the stories and beliefs around Modron

which help give depth to our understanding of her. Truly essential reading for anyone curious about Modron or who is drawn to the wider concept of mother goddesses
Morgan Daimler, author of *The Morrigan* and *Brigid*

An intriguing book exploring Modron as a figure, her myths and how these might relate to other 'Celtic' goddesses. This is ecologically solid writing that means to inspire not only relationships with this Goddess but also better relationships between humans and the land. Very relevant for anyone on the Druid path.
Nimue Brown, Druid, author of *Druidry and the Ancestors* and blogger

This is a fascinating book chock-filled with myth anchored by the Goddess Modron. Kelle is a lively storyteller diving into these epic and important tales. She also outlines rituals and invocations that allow a reader to plug into the energies she describes. A mythical journey that we can all partake of and a wonderful read.
Janet Rudolph, Co-Weaver of Feminism and Religion and author of *When Eve Was a Goddess* and *Desperately Seeking Persephone*

Pagan Portals

Modron

Meeting the Celtic Mother Goddess

Pagan Portals

Modron

Meeting the Celtic Mother Goddess

Kelle BanDea

MOON
BOOKS

London, UK
Washington, DC, USA

CollectiveInk

First published by Moon Books, 2025
Moon Books is an imprint of Collective Ink Ltd.,
Unit 11, Shepperton House, 89 Shepperton Road, London, N1 3DF
office@collectiveinkbooks.com
www.collectiveinkbooks.com
www.moon-books.net

For distributor details and how to order please visit the 'Ordering' section on our website.

ISBN: 978 1 80341 718 9
978 1 80341 734 9 (ebook)
Library of Congress Control Number: 2023950499

A CIP catalogue record for this book is available from the British Library.

Design: Lapiz Digital Services

UK: Printed and bound by CPI Group (UK) Ltd, Croydon, CR0 4YY
Printed in North America by CPI GPS partners

Contents

In memory of Emma Marie Quinn and Sylvie Palmer.
Sleep well in the Summerlands.

Introduction

Meeting the Mother

Mother of Gods, great nurse of all, draw near, divinely honored, and regard my prayer:

... earth is thine, and needy mortals share their constant food, from thy protecting care:

From thee at first both Gods and men arose; from thee, the sea and every river flows.

... source of good, thy name we find to mortal men rejoicing to be kind;

For every good to give, thy soul delights; come, mighty power, propitious to our rites,

All-taming, blessed, Phrygian savior, come, Saturn's great queen, rejoicing in the drum.

Celestial, ancient, life-supporting maid, fanatic Goddess, give thy suppliant aid

(from the Orphic hymn 'Meter Theon' or 'Mother of Gods' approx. 2BC)

Sometimes Deity takes us by surprise. Although I have had a pagan and pantheistic practice for some years now, and have worked as a celebrant and spiritual counselor, I previously had never felt drawn to the notion of a mother goddess, preferring a more abstract concept of Deity, or more 'glamorous' goddesses such as Aphrodite or Freya. Even when I became a mother myself – three times! – I still never connected to any of the goddesses associated with the mother aspect, in spite of the fact that being a mother was and is my biggest joy. In terms of my spiritual practice, it just wasn't something that felt right to me. Perhaps that came from a Christian upbringing with a parental Father god, or an antagonistic relationship with my own mother, but either way, me and the Great Mother were on acquaintance terms at best.

Then I visited Madron Well in Cornwall. I knew little of its folklore or connections with Modron/Matrona, only that it was considered a pagan site and a 'holy well' and I loved the sound of the name, which seemed to echo in my mind like a refrain. Or a call.

Next to the well, standing under the clootie tree, I had a subtle yet undeniably powerful spiritual experience which changed my practice forever, leaving me dedicated to this Celtic mother goddess, and with a passion to find out everything I could about her and incorporate it into my practice.

This book is the result. In it, I share what I have learned about Modron and her Gaulish equivalent, Matrona, as well as her association with other Welsh and Celtic goddesses, and even Arthurian legends. Chapter 1 will give an overview of her aspects and myths, while Chapter 2 will focus on her Christianisation into St Madryn and on Madron Well itself. In Chapter 3 I look at Modron's association with the Otherworld in both ancient and modern myth, and invite you to try a guided journey to meet her in the imaginal realm.

In Part II I will deep dive into some of her aspects and share practices for connecting with her in ritual and journeying and calling on her for healing of both ourselves and the land. We will discuss incorporating her into the neopagan Wheel of the Year – while also considering if she hasn't in fact been there all along – and suggestions for altars and invocations, as well as an example of a dedication ritual for those who would like to continue a personal exploration with her. Three chapters will focus on her main aspects in turn; her connection with motherhood and matriliny, water and healing, and guardianship of the land. As a face of the Great Mother, I will discuss drawing upon Modron for both fertility and loss, and also discuss the Motherline and her aspect as Ancestral Mother. Then we turn to her role as Sovereignty, as goddess of river and land, and look at what messages she may have for us today.

Modron has often been a somewhat shadowy figure in modern Celtic spirituality and neopaganism, but I believe her time has come. I hope you find this aspect of the Goddess as fascinating as I do.

Blessed be.

Part I

Meeting the Great Mother

Chapter 1

The Myths of Modron

In the realm of Celtic mythology, the goddess Modron is something of an obscure figure at first glance, and so is often not given the attention she deserves. Modron's mythological persona is shrouded in mystery, which may give a sense of allure and intrigue, or may simply result in her being overlooked. To truly understand her place in the pantheon of Celtic and specifically Brythonic deities, and her significance in neopagan and eco spiritualities, we must delve into the rich tapestry of myth and legend that surrounds her.

Throughout the Celtic world, as we shall see, Modron took on different aspects and roles. She could be a grieving mother, a guardian of the land, or a triplicity of goddesses, a symbol of both the deep mysteries of existence and of everyday matters, such as the harvest. The multiplicity of her character reflects the complexity of Celtic spirituality in general, where deities often embodied various aspects of life and nature, and simultaneously of death and the Otherworld. Celtic deities rarely fit neatly into boxes and Modron is no exception.

As we continue our exploration of Modron, it's essential to keep these mythological foundations in mind. Her multifaceted nature and her connections to other figures in Celtic mythology will become apparent as we dive further into her significance in both history and modern pagan practice. For as I hope to show, Modron is none other than a representation – perhaps *the* representation – of the great Celtic Mother Goddess, associated with fertility, sovereignty, the cycles of life and death and the Otherworld.

Modron is known to us both by her medieval myths, and from statues and inscriptions that go back to the turn of the century, where her name is rendered as Matrona. Although the tales we have about her are found predominantly in Brythonic and Welsh literature, and the statues and inscriptions found in Gaul and Northern England, when examined, the links between the two become obvious. For while definitive archaeological and historic proof is always hard to come by, there seems little doubt that Modron/Matrona, along with her son Mabon/ Maponus, was venerated over a large area. In fact, far from being a minor deity, a mere afterthought to the more popular Celtic goddesses such as Rhiannon or the Morrigan, she may in fact predate and even inspire aspects of their legends. She has been both syncretised into the Roman pantheon and absorbed into the legends of Christian saints, and offers many sites, landmarks and churches that can be visited in pilgrimage to her.

One of the most famous tales in which Modron is first encountered is found within the Welsh *Mabinogi*, a collection of medieval Welsh myths and legends, which scholars largely agree contain elements of more ancient Celtic myths, consisting of tales that were first told in oral form. In the *Mabinogi of Pwyll,* also known as the First Branch, we encounter her in passing as the mother of the legendary hero named Mabon, whose name means simply 'son' or 'youth.' His full title is often given as Mabon ap Modron, or 'son of the mother.' Scholars, particularly those of a Jungian slant, often see this as an indication that both Mabon and Modron are portrayals of the archetypes of the Great Mother and the Eternal or Divine Youth, which show up in mythology across the Western world. (Matthews, 2002)

In this tale, the Mother's son is taken from her at birth and later saved and returned, illustrating themes of exile, separation and reunion that echo through many other Celtic tales, particularly that of Rhiannon and Pryderi, as explored below.

The hero of the tale, Culhwch, embarks on a journey to find Mabon and seek his aid in his quest to win the hand of Olwen, a beautiful maiden whose father has imposed a series of seemingly impossible tasks as conditions for her hand in marriage.

Culhwch's journey to find Mabon causes him to encounter various figures from Welsh mythology, including Arthur and his knights. Along the way, Culhwch seeks their assistance and gathers companions for his quest, as in a traditional Hero's Journey. It becomes evident that Mabon is a key figure in helping to complete the tasks set by Olwen's father.

As the quest unfolds, it is revealed that Mabon has been imprisoned in a formidable Otherworld fortress since his infancy. The fortress is surrounded by steep cliffs and guarded by fierce animals, making it nearly impregnable. Nevertheless, Culhwch and his companions are determined to rescue Mabon. Although the fortress is described as Otherworldly, it is also stated in the *Triads* as being situated along the River Severn in Gloucester, and Mabon is described in the *Triads* as one of three 'Exalted' or 'Divine' Prisoners, indicating that the motif of the imprisoned or exiled hero/son is a significant one.

Arthur and his knights, known for their bravery and prowess, assist Culhwch in his perilous endeavor. With their combined strength, they breach the fortress, free Mabon, and bring him back to the world.

Mabon, upon his rescue, plays a crucial role in helping Culhwch complete the tasks set by Olwen's father, including the hunting of the fearsome boar, the Twrch Trwyth. His knowledge and superior hunting abilities are instrumental in achieving success in this challenge, because he is the only man who can hunt the dog Drudwyn; the only dog who can bring down the Twrch Trwyth. As the story says,

> *There is no hunter in the world who can handle that dog except Mabon son of Modron, who was taken from his mother when he was three nights old. No-one knows where he is, or what he is; whether he is alive or dead.*

Myths featuring hunts are some of the oldest known (Witzel, 2013) and the various animals featured in the story have echoes of ancient shamanic practices. The theme of a quest which involves various tests is also found in Classical as well as Celtic mythology. Ultimately, the successful completion of these tests leads to Culhwch's marriage to Olwen. There are echoes in this tale of a far older myth, perhaps, given the hunting and wild animal motifs, one that is potentially pre Indo-European and pre Neolithic.

The tale of Mabon and Modron in *Culhwch and Olwen* encapsulates several themes common in Celtic mythology, including the hero's journey, the rescue of a hidden or lost figure, and the interplay between the human and divine realms. Mabon's role as the Great Mother's son and his subsequent rescue from the Otherworld underscore the cyclical nature of life, death, and rebirth – a recurring theme in Celtic myth and indeed, mythology the world over. His kidnapping from his mother's side is significant, as seen by the repeated question asked by Culhwch and his men as they look for him; 'Do you know anything of Mabon son of Modron, who was taken on the third night from between his mother and the wall?' The repetition of this mysterious and somewhat eerie phrase indicates that there is something important about this story and about Mabon, beyond his usefulness to Culhwch.

Yet Modron herself is barely featured in this myth of her more famous son, mentioned only by name – or title. What then, can we take from this?

As mentioned above, there are significant parallels between this story of Modron and that of the well-known and beloved Welsh Goddess Rhiannon. One of Rhiannon's tales in the First Branch of the *Mabinogi* is so similar that some scholars, such as William John Gruffydd (1953) equate them as one figure, with 'Modron' being a designation of the goddess' role as Mother rather than a name in itself. Gruffydd also put forward the theory that this motif of the stolen child of the Goddess is one that may derive from an ancient, Proto-Indo-European myth, by comparing it with Classical myths that feature stolen divine children, such as that of Demeter and Persephone. It is certainly difficult to miss that Demeter is etymologically similar to Modron's older name, Dea Matrona (Divine Great Mother).

Like Modron, Rhiannon loses her son when he is newly born, although the story of Rhiannon and Pryderi is full of rich detail that the story of Modron and Mabon lacks. Pryderi disappears and his nursemaids, afraid of being punished, frame Rhiannon for his murder. Rhiannon protests her innocence, and her husband the king bizarrely condemns her to act as a beast of burden outside the castle gates, offering to carry visitors on her back. Eventually Pryderi returns after his own adventures, and Rhiannon is restored to her throne.

As well as the themes of separation and reunion between mother and son – and, in the case of Rhiannon, of restored justice – both tales involve traditional quests and hero's tales. Pryderi is a central figure in the *Mabinogi* and has been associated with Mabon ap Modron, sometimes, as with Rhiannon and Modron, believed to be the same figure.

Because of her association with horses (she initially appears as a woman from the Otherworld on a white horse) Rhiannon has also been associated with other Celtic horse goddesses such as Epona and also Rigantona, an epithet meaning 'divine queen.' John T Koch, an American historian, linguist and the author of *Celtic Culture; a Historical Encyclopaedia* (2005) believes the name Rhiannon to derive directly from Rigantona, and then goes on to equate Rigantona with Matrona ('great mother') and therefore Modron, further illustrating a potential link between Rhiannon and Modron, as well as our first hint here that Modron is synonymous with the more well-known goddess Matrona.

Modron has been solidly – and etymologically – linked to the Romano-Celtic mother goddess Matrona, who also has a divine son, Maponus, again cognate with Mabon. Maponus also means 'son' or 'youth' and Matrona is the Great Mother. Her name is, according to Noemie Beck (2015) unmistakably Celtic, deriving from the Gaulish 'matir' and cognate with the Old Irish 'mathair.' Both originate from the Indo-European 'mater.'

Matrona was a prominent figure in ancient Gaul and various dedications to Maponus are also found in ancient Britain, particularly along the site of the wall of Hadrian where he seems to have been particularly beloved by soldiers, as well as depictions of triple mother goddesses known as the Matronae or the Matres. A figure that resembles figures of Matrona has also been found here, although it is without a name.

Many inscriptions and artifacts dedicated to Matrona herself have been found throughout the Celtic/Gallic regions, particularly in what is now modern-day France and Germany, offering tangible evidence of widespread veneration of a Mother Goddess, including in a triple aspect as the three Matronae. This triple goddess symbolized three mother figures rather than the Maiden, Mother and Crone that neopagans may expect.

Matrona symbolized fertility and abundance, being typically shown with nursing babies, children, baskets of fruit, bread and cornucopias.

While her name and attributes suggest a universal Celtic/Gallic mother figure, it's important to acknowledge that Matrona will have taken on regional variations and nuances in her veneration; such as the Welsh Modron, for example. Nevertheless, the widespread archaeological findings associated with Matrona's cult indicate an enduring popularity and integral role for this goddess in the daily lives and spiritual beliefs of the Celtic peoples in ancient Gaul.

Matrona was also absorbed into Roman syncretism, where Roman deities were linked to the deities of the peoples they had colonized, and as such local deities may in some areas have taken on the attributes of Roman goddesses. She is usually referred to as 'Dea Matrona' and in the same fashion Maponus is often 'Apollo Maponus,' including in the Brythonic North of England and along Hadrian's Wall.

In Tongeren, Belgium, an altar dedicated to Matrona was found with an inscription that reads "To the mother goddesses and Matrona". The Museum of Saint-Germain-en-Laye in France houses numerous inscriptions and artifacts dedicated to Matrona. These inscriptions depict her with attributes of fertility, such as baskets of fruit, again underlining her role as a maternal figure associated with the Earth, abundance and prosperity.

The Matronae statues are a collection of around 1,100 sculptures discovered mainly in the Rhineland of Germany, an area that was once part of the ancient Gaulish or Celtic territory. These sculptures typically feature groups of three goddesses, sitting or standing together. They hold various symbols, including, once again, baskets of fruit, cornucopias, and babies, symbolizing fertility, abundance and protection. As stated above, the Matronae are described as the 'Three Mothers' or as sister goddesses rather than the more modern motif of Maiden, Mother and Crone, but historian Rudolf Simek (1996) notes that in some reliefs, the goddesses do show different attributes; for example, one goddess has loose hair which may suggest a maiden, whereas the other two have matronly headdresses. Snakes may also be depicted, which point to an association with healing, rebirth and the Otherworld. So while the Matronae do not easily fit into the Maiden, Mother, Crone categories, there are suggestions that the three goddesses sometimes vary in age and/or function. In this, they occupy a similar space as other triple goddesses; the Norns, the Fates, the Hindu Tridevi and, of course, the three faces of the Morrigan. Simek also suggests that the presence of children and babies show they may have been considered midwives as well as mother figures, and were likely called upon, in a time of high infant and maternal mortality, for success in childbirth.

While her associations with the fertility of the Earth and abundance are clear, Matrona/Modron also has a strong association with healing wells, beyond the well in Madron, Cornwall where I first encountered her. Inscriptions and depictions of Matrona and the Matronae are also typically found near springs, rivers and wells, and therefore she can be viewed as a Goddess of water and healing as well as of the land. In fact, the two are often intimately entwined, and point to an association with Sovereignty.

Sovereignty has to do with stewardship of the land, and with kingship or leadership. In many Celtic myths and in the later Arthurian tradition, an Otherworldly woman grants kingship to a worthy hero, which ties his fate intimately to the fate of the land. If he fails to look after the land and its people, kingship is revoked. Sovereignty figures are often associated with water sources, and may offer the hero a drink or platter as symbolic of the granting of Sovereignty and the abundance of the land. This was later associated with the Grail. Many Celtic figures have been associated with Sovereignty, including Rhiannon herself, the Morrigan, and characters such as the Lady of the Lake in the Arthurian tales. Celtic scholar Sharon Paice MacLeod (2018) has explored in depth how this idea as the Goddess as Sovereignty underlies much of Celtic mythology and may have very deep and old roots. In this view, the Mother is the Sovereignty figure, and the Mabon is the hero who receives her blessing, after being tested to prove his worth.

Another tale in the *Mabinogi* is that of Lleu Llaw Gyffes (often equated with Lugh in the Irish myths) who is also separated from his mother, the goddess Arianrhod. In this story, however, Arianrhod abandons rather than grieves her baby, and puts a geis (taboo or curse) on him so he cannot be named, bear arms or marry, which Lleu finds his way around with the help of his uncle, the magician Gwydion. This power to deny her son a name and lineage reveals Arianrhod to be a figure of Sovereignty.

The other main female figure in the *Mabinogi* is Branwen, sister of Bran, who has a tragic tale, and whose son Gwern – supposed to be the future High King of Ireland, bringing two peoples together – is actually killed. Her story also has parallels with that of Rhiannon in that Branwen is falsely accused and persecuted, and she is also associated with Sovereignty. As the grieving mother, Branwen eventually dies of a broken heart.

And, of course, we have the much-loved tale of Cerridwen from the 14th century Welsh manuscript, the *Book of Taliesin*. Cerridwen is the keeper of the Cauldron of Awen ('flowing spirit,' a Celtic concept which is somewhat similar to the Eastern Tao and is the source of inspiration for bards) who births the bard Taliesin after swallowing Gwion Bach, who steals drops of Awen from her cauldron. She then puts the baby Taliesin adrift on the sea. Like Arianrhod, she is depicted as an initiatory goddess of Sovereignty.

All of these Brythonic Welsh mother figures share some similarities; they are all associated with Sovereignty, and all have sons who are destined to be kings or bards, whom they are, for various reasons, separated from while this son is still a baby. While some disagree, citing the obvious differences in their stories, other scholars state that not just Rhiannon and Pryderi, but all of these prominent mothers and sons are facets of Modron and Mabon. Patrick Ford, in his 1977 translation of the *Mabinogi*, has offered the thesis that the title 'Mabinogi' refers to the tales or stories of Mabon, a thesis which many modern neopagans find convincing. (Hughes 2013) Whatever the truth of it, there is little doubt that this motif of the divine mother and her famous son was a widespread and important one.

Gruffydd, as mentioned above, equates this motif to Classical myth, and believes that Modron/Matrona and Mabon/Maponus were originally part of a mythic tale that is lost to us but which equates to the myth of Demeter, and is linked to the turning of the seasons; to the abundance of summer giving way to the scarcity of winter. The child is taken from the mother, leading her to grieve and the land to become the Wasteland of winter. When the child is returned, fertility returns to the land and spring comes once again.

While Gruffydd may seem to be stretching here, there is some hint of this in the *Mabinogi;* in the Third branch, which has further tales of Rhiannon and Pryderi, the land is depicted as becoming a Wasteland while Pryderi suffers a further imprisonment, although this is never explicitly linked to the turning of the seasons. This is intriguing, but it is important to remember that the *Mabinogi* was written later and so may have absorbed influences from Classical myth, rather than this being indicative of a shared Proto Indo-European root. As no early myth of Matrona and Maponus survives, all we have is educated guesswork and the piecing together of fragments of myth with little proof as to how the similarities arose. A Jungian scholar may say that there is a shared myth, but one which arose from the collective unconscious (the realm of archetypes) with no need for syncretism or shared ancient roots. Those with a more sociological analysis may well point out that the turning of the seasons, from the abundance of harvest to the famine of winter, would have been a matter of life and death to various cultures, and so perhaps similar stories are to be expected.

Regardless of a potential link with the Demeter tale, the Wasteland is a common motif in Celtic mythology, one which is more typically attributed to the notions of Sovereignty and stewardship of the land as discussed above. This is something I will return to in the next chapter and later in this book.

While all this is fascinating (at least to me!) it still leaves Modron herself as that shadowy figure, as an overarching archetype or ancestral figure rather than a specific deity with her own myth and place in the Brythonic Celtic mythological cycle. While others may interpret her this way, I have a perception of her as a distinct goddess, rather than merely a title which can encompass all others, and indeed she does have her own myth, separate from those of Rhiannon and others, which still retains many similar attributes.

The *Welsh Triads* give us more details about her, ones which equate her both with the legendary King Urien (and therefore the region of Cumbria and the Brythonic Old North of England) and with the Otherworldly land of Annwn, as well as introducing other motifs such as the Washer at the Ford.

Triad 70 introduces her with: *Three Heroic Bards of the Isle of Britain: Urien Rheged, Taliesin, and Modron daughter of Afallach.* The *Triads* then tell us that Modron, daughter of Afallach, was the mother of the twins Owain and Morfydd by Urien of Rheged. Another Welsh manuscript fragment, known as Peniarth 147 then gives us a fuller story, which I have paraphrased here:

> *The ancient realm of Rheged was once ruled by the legendary King Urien, a wise and powerful ruler known for his prowess in battle and cattle-raiding, and his commitment to justice. Urien's reputation extended far and wide, and his name was respected throughout the land.*
>
> *One day, as Urien was traveling through his kingdom, he came upon a ford where it was said that all the hounds of the country often gathered to bark. No-one was brave enough to see what was causing the barking, except Urien himself. He approached the ford only to find a washerwoman kneeling, diligently washing clothes in the river. Her appearance was unremarkable, but there was something about her demeanor that caught Urien's attention. She seemed to exude an air of otherworldly wisdom and mystery.*
>
> *Approaching the washerwoman, Urien struck up a conversation with her, and seduced her. Afterwards, the woman blessed him and told him that she had been fated to wash at the ford until she*

should bear two children, a boy and a girl, to a Christian king. She then revealed herself to be none other than the daughter of Afallach, the King of Annwn, the Otherworld.

She foretold a son of great valor and a daughter of unsurpassed beauty and grace, and a year later Urien returned to the ford to collect his children. His son, Owain, grew into a fearless and renowned warrior, while his daughter, Morfudd, became celebrated for her exceptional beauty.

There is a lot to unpack here. The washerwoman at the ford is an archetypal figure in Celtic folklore across the Brythonic (Welsh, Cornish and Breton) and Goidelic (Irish and Scottish) lands, and one who is more commonly associated with death than with birth. She is typically described as a mysterious woman who appears at a river or ford, where she is engaged in the eerie and Otherworldly task of washing bloody clothes or armor. These garments are often believed to be omens of impending doom or death in battle. She has been associated with the Irish war and death goddess the Morrigan, and is also known in Scottish folklore as the Bean Nighe, an Otherworldly figure who washes the bloody clothes of those slain, or about to be slain, in battle. In some stories of the Bean Nighe, rather than a faery or divine figure, she is the spirit of a woman who died in childbirth. She is sometimes described as being ugly in appearance, with one nostril, tusk-like teeth and webbed feet, and she can be petitioned for three wishes.

These depictions of the Bean Nighe as ugly are reminiscent of the Loathly Lady, or Cundrie, in Arthurian mythology, who is typically revealed to be a Goddess of Sovereignty and of the land – revealing further echoes of Modron, or the Great Mother, Matrona. The ford itself is a representation, like a crossroads, of a liminal or 'thin' place, where the boundary between our world and the Otherworld is thin. In this sense the washer at the ford may be viewed as a threshold guardian, as well as, like the Bean Sidhe (banshee) a harbinger of death.

The washer woman at the ford is also associated with tales of the Morrigan, one of the most complex and enigmatic figures in Celtic mythology. Morrigan is an Irish goddess of war, fate, and Sovereignty, and she is known for her shape-shifting abilities, including as a raven or crow, symbolic of her prophetic powers and her role as a chooser of the slain. The washer woman of the bloody garments is also sometimes named as Badb, one of the triple faces of the Morrigan.

Although the washer woman story suggests a link between the Morrigan and Modron, perhaps as faces of the Life/Death nature of the Goddess, the link is somewhat tenuous. It has been strengthened in modern times by the fact that they are both associated with the Arthurian figure of Morgan le Fay. In Arthurian legend, Morgan is both depicted as the Queen of Avalon and the wife of Urien (and sometimes mother of Owain) and as the Lady of the Lake at the head of the Avalonian barge which carries away Arthur's body. She is associated with both death and sorcery, and in some tales is Arthur's adversary (and sister) rather than guide, assisting in the final battle against him. Her epithet 'le Fay' indicates that she is a woman of the Otherworld.

There are various renditions of the story of Morgan, and they become more detailed over time. The earliest is the most similar to the tale of Modron, found in the *Vita Merlina,* written by Geoffrey of Monmouth, (1150) wherein Morgan is the wife of a character called Uriens, and is from the Isle of Apples – Annwn/Avalon, or the Otherworld. In Chrétien de Troyes *Perceval* (1180–90) she is first given the epithet 'le Fay' and is now Arthur's sister, with a son called Owein. In Ulrich von Zatzikhoven's *Lanzelet* (1194), the son of the Lady of the Lake is called Mabuz, which has been suggested as a rendition of

Mabon. It seems fairly likely then that Modron served as at least part of the inspiration for the literary character of Morgan.

These links are enigmatic but elusive, although often popular in modern paganism, particularly the idea of Morgan as an Arthurian counterpart to the Morrigan, which seems to have no real substance to it other than shared correspondences, and likely comes through their shared similarities to Modron rather than any actual link to one another. Nevertheless it is a popular perception, and I have also seen some neopagan practitioners use Morgan, Modron and the Morrigan as the faces of the neopagan triple goddess; Maiden, Mother and Crone. Myths continue to evolve and to flourish, making them living traditions rather than simply relics of the past.

In the tale of the ford, Modron is not just a mythical figure or Otherworldly deity but a woman who enters into history – or at least pseudo-history. King Urien of Rheged and his son Owain are historical figures, although much of the tales about them, particularly those that have been absorbed into Arthurian legend, are fantastical. Inserting Modron into the royal family gives Owain a special lineage, in much the same way as the Tudors claimed to be descended from King Arthur and the Roman Caesars to have become demi-gods.

So far, then, we have seen the figure of Modron evolve from a Celtic-Romano mother goddess, perhaps originally a regional deity associated with the river Marne, whose widespread veneration is archaeologically attested to but about whose myths we know little, other than that she was associated with motherhood and the land and sometimes depicted as a triplicity, and was closely associated with her son, a Divine Youth figure likened by the Romans to Apollo. We then see her again briefly mentioned in the *Mabinogi*, where her story has parallels with that of other, more detailed tales, especially that of Rhiannon. Finally, we see that she has a myth of her own, one which sees her cross the realm from divinity into contact with the mortal world by becoming consort and mother to the pseudo-historical figures of Urien of Rheged and his heroic son, Owain. This myth and its characters have been absorbed into the Arthurian stories, where Modron has at least partially inspired the character of Morgan le Fay.

This is quite a lot of material, but it is still not all. Modron, like other prominent Celtic goddesses, such as the Irish Brigid, may have become a Christian saint, and some aspects of her veneration remain today.

Chapter 2

Saint Madryn and Madron Well

One of the most noteworthy aspects of Matrona's worship is her association with water. Springs, rivers, and wells were considered sacred in Celtic belief, possessing both purifying and healing qualities. Matrona was often connected to water sources, signifying a role as a guardian of the life-giving element. (This may hint at a further association with Morgan as the Lady of the Lake.) She is also, and more commonly, associated with the River Marne in France, where her cult is generally assumed to have originated.

An inscription found on a second century altar in Balesme-sur-Marne reads:

> *Successus, freed from Natalis, had this outer wall of rubble stones built around this temple at his own expense in honor of Matrona, after making a vow, and paid his vow willingly and deservedly.*

The inscription is believed to refer to a temple which was built a few kilometers away at the spring of the river. The ruins show it had twelve rooms and hot baths, indicating it was a curative spa. (Beck, 2015)

Water sources and wells were considered not only as sources of physical healing but also as places where the divine and the natural world intersected. Matrona's presence at these wells hint at a further role as a guardian of life, health, and well-being. A prominent example is found in Bourbonne-les-Bains, France, where inscriptions and offerings have been found, showing she was associated with the thermal springs there, which were believed to have curative properties.

Pilgrims and worshippers sought her intercession for physical healing, protection, and overall well-being, believing that the waters imbued with her divine presence held the power to restore health and vitality.

These practices didn't die out with the advent of Christianity but rather became absorbed, with 'holy wells' being dedicated to various saints, many of which are thinly veiled Christianised versions of Celtic/Gaulish deities. Many scholars see an obvious continuation of the worship of a mother goddess in the cult of the Virgin Mary, the Mother of God, and the Divine Son, making Mary and Jesus possibly another example of the 'mother and son' deities which Mobon/Matrona and Mabon/Maponus exemplify. Caitlin Matthews (2002) makes this explicit, giving further weight to the idea of a widespread shared myth.

The Madron Well, also known as St. Madern's Well or St. Maddern's Well, has a rich and storied history that dates back many centuries and appears to be a good example of a Christianised pagan sacred site. Its origins are believed to be pre-Christian, with the well initially serving as a sacred site before the advent of Christianity in the British Isles.

According to local history, the well is named after St. Madern (or Madron), a 6th-century Celtic Christian saint who resided in the area. It is said that St. Madern was renowned for his healing abilities and that he used the waters of the well to cure ailments and provide comfort to the afflicted. The well subsequently became associated with his name and legacy.

However, there is so little information available about St. Madern that it has been suggested by scholars that he never existed at all. Others have suggested he was a hermit from Brittany who was born in Cornwall, but this seems odd, given that the site of the well is not where he lived and therefore he could hardly dispense cures from its water. It is perhaps more likely that he has been confused with a female saint of a similar name, St Madryn. Another suggestion, most commonly accepted by the pagan community, is that 'Madron' is another rendering of Modron or Matrona, the Mother Goddess. When we look at the stories of St. Madryn, this seems likelier still.

St. Madryn (also written Modrun and Madron) was, according to her legend, the granddaughter of Vortigern, whose name means 'great king.' The writings of the early medieval clerics St. Bede and Gildas from the sixth century record him as being a fifth century warlord, who took refuge in North Wales. According to Christian legend, as recorded by Sabine Baring-Gould (1914) while on a pilgrimage to Bardsey Island, Madryn had an angelic vision or dream which inspired her to build a church. There are various churches dedicated to her, and a Castle Madryn in the South Llyn Peninsula. The castle is close to various sites with a dedication to Madryn in their names, including Carn Fadryn (Fort of Madrun). The fort, however, long predates the time in which Madryn is believed to have lived.

Like other early Christian saints, it is likely that Madryn is a later depiction of the goddess Modron/Matrona, or at least that the saint's legend has become entwined with that of the goddess. She may also possibly have been named after her. Another story of Madryn has her fleeing Saxon soldiers with her newly born son, (another mother with a threatened baby son) and relocating to Cornwall. As well as the parish of Madron and Madron Well itself, there are two churches dedicated to her, one in Boscastle and one very close to Tintagel. The Boscastle church has another holy well dedicated to her.

Madryn is believed to have been the granddaughter of Vortigern, and the southern Llyn Peninsula has a variety of place names believed to be associated with Vortigern, as well as his holy granddaughter. Vortigern is another pseudo-historical figure, believed to be King of the Britons from 425-450, when Britain was under threat from the Saxon kings Hengist and Horsa. Vortigern allied with Hengist and Horsa against the

Picts and the Scots, rewarding them with land, for which he was later berated in the early medieval texts of St Gildas and the Venerable Bede, who believed him to be a pagan tyrant who was advised by his wizards, although Geoffrey of Monmouth later claimed him as a Christian. According to the 14th century compilation *Genealogy of the Saints* his granddaughter Madryn married Ynyr Honorius, the King of Gwent. Thus the saint, as well as the goddess, is given royal lineage. She then becomes the mother of Caradoc, who is later King of South Wales. Caradoc is sometimes listed as Arthur's cousin and as a Knight of the Round Table – as is Owain, son of Modron. At the very least, it seems the stories and place names associated with Modron and Madryn have become intertwined.

Cornwall also has a parish called St. Mabyn, with an accompanying church. In an interesting twist, St. Mabyn was a female. However, Sabine Baring-Gould in *Lives of the Saints* (1914) believes Mabyn to have actually been a Welsh male saint. One called Mabon.

Teasing out the exact truth and historical origin of each of these references may be impossible today, but we know enough to at least strongly suggest the widespread veneration of a mother goddess (and sometimes three goddesses) known as Modron/Matrona and her divine son Mabon/Maponus, across both England and Wales and Gaul. The goddess then became Christianised (and we can see some of the Christian gloss in the tale of Modron and Urien at the ford) and like so many, became entwined with the Christian saints. While this Christianisation served to obscure pagan origins of figures such as Modron, it also inadvertently helped preserve their veneration, and many of the sites of once-pagan saints became Christian sites of both worship and prayer, particularly for healing.

Madron Well is certainly renowned for its healing properties. Pilgrims and visitors still come from far and wide to visit the waters, even though the well is now little more than a trickle, believing that they hold the power to cure a variety of ailments, both physical and spiritual. Historically, Madron used to supply water for the entire parish (also called Madron) in a tangible example of the goddess' abundance.

The act of dipping oneself in the well's waters or tying offerings to nearby trees or bushes (often strips of fabrics known as 'clooties' which are believed to rot as the pain or illness subside) was both a form of devotion and a means of invoking the healing energies of the water.

Surrounding the well today are several trees adorned with colorful ribbons and cloth strips, showing that the clootie tradition is alive and well and still an integral part of the holy well veneration. Visitors still tie their offerings to the trees while making wishes or seeking blessings. This practice is reminiscent of similar traditions found at other sacred sites in the Celtic world, from stone circles to sacred groves.

Just a little way up the path from the clootie trees and the wellhead is a ruined chapel, a scheduled Ancient Monument believed to date as far back as the 12th century, dedicated to the elusive St Madern. Take a visit to it today and you're still likely to find homemade temporary altars set up there, consisting of flowers or other offerings, showing the site is very much still in use. On my own trips there, I find the chapel feels as powerful energetically as the well itself, and I am not surprised so many visitors are drawn there, whether pagan, Christian or anything else.

When we visit or make pilgrimages to such sites, we are reminded that these places are not merely relics of the past but living symbols of our enduring quest for the Divine and the miraculous in the world around us. Madron Well continues to offer its healing embrace to all who seek it, reminding us that some things are timeless, regardless of who we dedicate them to at any given time.

Madron was also the site of Britain's last living well keeper, An Katty. The tradition of well keeping has deep roots in British culture and history, just as the wells themselves have held a special place in the hearts and minds of local people and pilgrims for centuries.

Well keepers, often local individuals and typically women, were sometimes found at holy wells, helping to supply 'cures' and to pray for the sick. It was a tradition frowned upon as pagan by local clergy and as a superstition after the Enlightenment, but local legends suggest that at one time these custodians of the sacred waters were integral to the community and held a position of respect and responsibility.

For some, well keepers were seen as mediators between the earthly realm and the supernatural. They were thought to have a special connection to the spirits or deities associated with the well and could offer prayers, blessings, or guidance to those seeking solace, healing, or divine favor.

An Katty is depicted in records from the 19th century (Bottrell, 1873) when the well and chapel were still regularly visited as sites of healing cures, especially for eye problems, skin diseases in children and back pain. It was also associated with divination, and An Katty is believed to have told fortunes there, especially for young women who visited on May Day, wanting to know about their marriage prospects. She refused to take money, instead requesting payments of yarn or food. She reportedly told Bottrell, a folklorist recording Cornish traditions, that she had no knowledge of any saint ever being associated with the well, that it was a 'Wishing Well' and the power came from there, not from the chapel. Needless to say, the local Anglican clergy disapproved of both her and the seasonal traditions. Later on in the century, Methodists started to hold services at the ruined chapel. But while the tradition of the well keeper may have died out, it may still offer something for a time in which our relationship with the land has never been more strained.

In Sharon Blackie's thought-provoking work, *If Women Rose Rooted,* (2016) she explores the figure of the well keeper or 'well maiden,' drawing parallels to what she sees as a profound connection between women and the land, portrayed in both ancient myths and contemporary ecofeminist narratives. One of the compelling stories within the book, adapted from a medieval myth in the *Elucidation,* is "The Rape of the Well Maidens," which Blackie believes sheds light on women's historical roles as guardians of the land and the impact of their connection to the earth, a poignant metaphor that intertwines the exploitation of the land with the oppression of women.

In this ecofeminist narrative, the well maidens represent the deep wisdom and life-giving essence of the earth. They are the guardians of the sacred springs and the keepers of ancient knowledge. As stewards of the land, they embody an intrinsic connection between women and the earth. The violation of the well maidens mirrors the historical and ongoing exploitation of the natural world and of women's bodies. Just as the land has been stripped of its resources and despoiled by human activities, women's wisdom and agency have often been suppressed and marginalized.

While I find much depth in this idea and appreciate Blackie's work, I do not think we need to limit this wisdom tale as only applying to women. Not only does this risk an essentialist narrative that risks constraining women's role, it also overlooks the fact that men and those with other gender identities have as much of a role to play in restoring humanity's relationship to the earth and to the Divine. Modron, after all, is rarely mentioned without Mabon, and vice versa.

The *Elucidation* itself was written by an anonymous thirteenth century author and was designed to serve as a sort of prequel to de Troyes' *Perceval, le Conte du Graal,* a fourteenth century French Arthurian tale. However, Wilder Thompson (1931) believes the poem has significant differences in meaning to *Perceval,* particularly in its last quarter. To briefly summarize, the poem warns the reader that secrets about the Grail are about to be revealed, which must be kept. It then recounts the story of the well maiden raped by King Amargon which Blackie retells as an ecofeminist narrative. Because of this crime, not only does the land become a barren Wasteland, but the Castle of the Fisher King can no longer be found. The Fisher King features in the Arthurian tale as a wounded king whose wounding brings barrenness to the land, and it is in Perceval that he is first encountered, although some scholars believe his origins lie in the tale of Bran, brother of Branwen in the *Mabinogi,* and his magical cauldron which resurrects the dead. The Fisher King is sometimes shown as wounded in the groin – a fitting punishment for the rape of the well maidens, perhaps? This is certainly what the *Elucidation* appears to imply.

The *Elucidation* then goes on to depict Arthur's knights defending maidens in battle who are discovered to be the descendants of the well maidens. Arthur then instructs his knights to find the court of the Fisher King. As in *Perceval,* it is the young knight Perceval who locates the castle and witnesses the 'Grail procession' where maidens carry the Grail as well as magical platters of food that are never emptied, signifying the abundance offered by the Grail. He also sees the Fisher King, who has a wound that does not heal. In *Perceval,* he fails to ask what is known as the Grail question 'Whom does the Grail serve?' and so the court vanishes. In the *Elucidation,* he does ask this question, but fails to ask another; 'What ails thee?' He does not ask the Fisher King about his wound, and so the court disappears, back into the Otherworld.

Both texts are considered difficult to understand by interpreters, and have wider meanings within the Arthurian cycle of tales that are not relevant here, but what the *Elucidation* does offer us is the tying of the well maidens to the Grail. The Grail has long been considered by both scholars and neopagans alike to have roots in Celtic myth that have nothing to do with Christian cups but which have more to do with the life giving waters offered by Sovereignty goddesses, or the magical cauldrons associated with figures such as Cerridwen. (Blackie, 2016)

Modron herself is more than a well maiden, but it is tempting to speculate that the figure of the Otherworldly well keeper was derived from goddesses such as her, with their association with both healing waters, overflowing cornucopias and baskets, and a Sovereignty function of legitimizing a king's reign. These motifs are far older than later Arthurian stories of the Holy Grail. Nevertheless we can see the similarities, carried through time.

Another motif, which is entwined with the figure of Modron, is that of the Otherworld.

Chapter 3

Modron and the Celtic Otherworld

In Chapter 1 we saw that Modron is identified as being an Otherworldly figure and the daughter of Afallach. But who is Afallach, and how does this parentage link Modron to the Brythonic Otherworld of Annwn and, in later legend, to Avalon?

The *Triads* list Afallach as one of the Kings of Annwn, the name of the Brythonic, and particularly Welsh, Otherworld, rendered in earlier sources as Annwfn, which roughly translates as 'deep place' or 'not-world.' Afallach's name means 'place of apples,' which also connects him with the Celtic Otherworld, as it was often associated with apples (Bromwich, 2008) particularly as an island with orchards or magical apple trees. Afallach also appears in some of the genealogies of Gwynedd in North Wales – an area which, as we saw in the last chapter, is linked with St Madryn.

Annwn, and the Celtic Otherworld in general, is sometimes depicted as being accessible through actual physical locations, and at other times as a sort of alternate dimension to our everyday world, which lies below or alongside our world, and is accessible at liminal times or states. For example, twilight, after drinking mead, during trance or meditation, or 'beyond the Ninth Wave.' It is both like and unlike our world, but does not conform to our rules around time and space. Folktales of humans who wander into the world of Faery for a night and then come back to find that years have passed are reminiscent of this quality. Enchanted islands also feature prominently and tales of them are found across the Celtic world, from the Irish Tir Na n'Og to the Isle of Ys in Brittany. Irish lore also tells us of Emain Ablach, or the 'place of apples' which has etymological ties to the name of Afallach.

Annwn itself has been depicted as containing many islands, as in the medieval Welsh poem 'Preiddeu Annwn,' or 'the Spoils of Annwn,' which features prominently in the *Book of Taliesin*, a compilation of poetry attributed to the legendary bard Taliesin. Although the manuscript itself dates from the thirteenth century, many scholars believe, due to linguistic analysis, that the 'Spoils of Annwn,' may date back as far as the sixth century (Lacy, 1991). The poem tells the tale of Arthur and his warriors raiding the Otherworld in order to steal a magical cauldron that belongs to the Chief of Annwn, and which is kept alight by the 'breath of Nine Maidens.' There are various island fortresses within this depiction of Annwn, and the journey is perilous, indicating that the Otherworld is not always a paradisiacal place – at least if one is entering it intent on theft! There is a parallel here between the tale of the well maidens that we touched on in the last chapter, suggesting an older root to this story. Arthur and his warriors attempt to bring violence to the Otherworld and its maidens and steal the life-giving vessel. Ultimately, the poem describes them as 'undeserving,' and many of the warriors die in the attempt, which also links the tale to the testing of Sovereignty (the poem also references Pwyll and Pryderi). It can also be read as an inner journey, with the different forts representing different trials in life or aspects of the subconscious (Hughes, 2013). It has also been suggested as a metaphor for the bardic quest of seeking the inspiration of Awen, which is brewed in an Otherworldly cauldron.

Whatever its meaning, the poem may be one of our earliest sources for the Otherworld as Annwn, and one of the many reasons that in recent times Annwn is often seen as synonymous with Avalon, even though many scholars dispute this.

Avalon, in the Arthurian tradition, is the Otherworldly isle on which lives Morgan le Fay, or sometimes the Lady of the Lake, and often nine maidens (Morgan being one of and the chief of these). The name Avalon is also etymologically linked with apples.

What does this have to do with Modron? Well, the name Avalon is believed to derive from Ynys Afallach, or the Isle of Afallach, the father of Modron and a king of Annwn. Afallach is also sometimes said to reside on his island with his daughters. From this, there is on the face of it an obvious link with Avalon as one of the islands on Annwn and Morgan as a literary rendering of Modron.

Avalon as we know it today, however, is largely a medieval invention, and we first encounter it in the writings of Geoffrey of Monmouth. In his *Historia* (1130) Avalon is mentioned as the island that Arthur was carried to after being mortally wounded, and is the place where his magical sword was forged. Later in the *Vita Merlini,* Avalon is referred to as the paradisiacal Island of Apples, and Morgen is first mentioned as the head of nine magical sisters. Morgen is described as a shapeshifter and incredibly powerful healer, and the lady who receives Arthur after being mortally wounded at the Battle of Camlann. Given the island's name and its link with apples and the mention of nine magical maidens, it is often suggested that Geoffrey was influenced by the tales of Annwn, particularly the 'Spoils,' just as the tales of Modron inspired the character of Morgen.

It is unlikely that this was the only influence, however. Geoffrey also compares Avalon directly with the Fortunate Isles of Classical tradition, which may suggest his nine maidens were directly inspired by the Classical Nine Muses, especially as Geoffrey describes one of them as being musically gifted. Avalon, as we know it in the Arthurian tradition, has likely arisen from a variety of influences and, of course, Geoffrey and later writers' imaginations. It is not simply a modern rendering of Annwn.

Nevertheless, in recent tradition the legend of Avalon has become an important one for many seekers, including neopagans and especially those inspired by or working with Brythonic tradition. As I stated earlier, myths change and evolve over time, retaining their core perhaps but taking on new garments and interpretations. While not directly synonymous with Annwn or any of the various depictions of the Celtic Otherworld, Avalon has become perhaps a specific part of it, accessible to those who believe in and work with its legend and the traditions inspired by it.

There have been various suggestions over the years for a specific location for Avalon over the years, including places in Brittany and Wales, but the most famous has to be that of Glastonbury, a town in Somerset, England, whose name has become virtually interchangeable with that of Avalon to many modern-day seekers. And for some of those seekers, Modron too can be found there.

Glastonbury has long been a place of pilgrimage, and is said to be the site of the first Christian church in England, and home to many legends about the child Jesus and Joseph of Arimathea, including one where Joseph buries the Holy Grail beneath Glastonbury Tor. It was also said to be the home of King Arthur's grave, although this is now generally recognised as a medieval forgery designed to bring prosperity and fame to Glastonbury Abbey. But even if King Arthur's grave wasn't real, there is no denying that Glastonbury is a magical place, and it is easy when one is there to imagine that the Otherworld and its denizens are very close indeed.

Although often considered the place where Christianity in England began, local lore states that Glastonbury may have been a site of pilgrimage that predates Christianity, and local features certainly make this highly likely. Chalice Well Gardens are home to the aptly named Red Spring, where an abundant wellspring bubbles up with water so rich in iron that it stains the rocks around it red. Close to it is the White Spring, where the water is full of calcium, staining the rocks white. These water sources must have seemed miraculous to our Celtic ancestors, and neopagans

nowadays may see them as symbolic of the Goddess (the Red Spring) and the God (the White Spring) or as the Goddess' blood and milk, symbols of her abundance. The White Spring lies at the bottom of the Tor, a hill ringed with seven terraces, the purpose of which are unknown but which form a natural walkway looping up and around the Tor. Local legend has it that another King of Annwn, Gwynn ap Nudd, lives in the caves underneath the Tor, and at certain times leads the Wild Hunt and his pack of Otherworldly hounds down from the top of the Tor.

Christians, pagans, and New Age seekers alike are regularly drawn to Glastonbury as Avalon, and it has fascinated magical practitioners over the years, including Dion Fortune, whose novel *The Sea Priestess* features Morgan le Fay as a character. It has been associated with ley lines, alternative zodiacs, Goddess Spirituality and Eastern wisdom (it is sometimes called the heart chakra of the Earth) as well as Christian and Arthurian legend. The weight of all this legend and association means that Avalon has perhaps become an integral part of how we can access the Otherworld, even if it originally had little to do with Annwn at all before the legends of Geoffrey of Monmouth.

Different 'Avalonian Traditions' now flourish, ones that often revolve around Celtic goddesses and priestess traditions, influenced by the tales of the Nine Maidens. Two of the most prominent actively include Modron among their lore. The Sisterhood of Avalon, created by Jhenah Telyndru, centers around the concept of the Nine Maidens and the Celtic Goddess as portrayed by the Otherworldly women of Welsh lore; Rhiannon, Arianrhod, Branwen and Cerridwen, as well as Morgan herself. In this tradition, Glastonbury's Chalice Hill is known as Modron's Mound, and is associated with the Awen and with the full moon. (Telyndru, 2010)

There is also the Glastonbury Goddess Temple, an official place of worship on Glastonbury High Street, founded by Kathy Jones who has also created a modern Priestess of Avalon tradition. Utilizing a Wheel of the Year that is constructed around a 'Goddess of Avalon,' Brythonic goddesses are again featured, including Modron, who is described as 'the Great Mother Madron or Modron, Mother of the lineage of Avallach, From whose dreaming womb, All that is new is brought to birth.' (Jones, 2021) Modron continues to be reimagined, remembered, and her veneration reclaimed and renewed.

The next part of this book will focus on ways of working with Modron, and so before we delve into this I invite you to try the guided journey below to meet her in the 'imaginal realm;' that place in our own subconscious where we might come into contact with the edge of the Otherworld. This is best read out by a trusted other, or recorded by yourself and played back. Leave a pause after each paragraph to fully absorb the experience. Don't worry if you haven't journeyed in this way before or find it difficult to visualize; this is worded in such a way as to guide you gently into a state of deep relaxation where you will find such journeying effortless. People often describe it as 'dreaming awake.' If you have ever visited a hypnotherapist, it is a similar experience.

A Script for a Guided Journey to Avalon to Meet the Otherworldly Mother

Find a comfortable position, sitting or lying down, in a place where you won't be disturbed. Gently close your eyes and take a deep breath in, slowly filling your lungs with air. As you exhale, imagine a warm, glowing light beginning to form above your head. This light is pure, serene, and filled with calming energy.

With another deep breath, allow this light to touch the top of your head, feeling a sense of relaxation beginning to spread across your scalp. The light is gentle, soothing, like a balm to your thoughts. With every exhale, it eases any tension in your forehead, your temples, and your eyes.

As the light glides down, your cheeks, jaw, and neck all begin to soften. Let the warmth dissolve any tightness as it moves steadily through your body. Your shoulders drop comfortably, a feeling of lightness taking over.

The warm light travels down your arms, relaxing your biceps, your elbows, your forearms, and into your wrists and hands. Each finger releases its hold, free from all strain.

With each breath, the light's tranquil journey continues down your chest and your upper back, easing the muscles, freeing your heart to beat calmly, rhythmically.

The warm light swirls around your abdomen and lower back, unwinding knots, relaxing every fiber.

It moves through your hips, your thighs, melting any heaviness as it descends, sweeping through your knees, your calves, your ankles. Each part of you becoming more relaxed, more at peace.

Finally, the light reaches your feet, and with it, every last bit of tension drains away. You are enveloped in warmth and relaxation, ready to begin your inner journey.

Imagine yourself standing atop a verdant hill just as twilight descends. The sky above is a tapestry of deep blues and purples, the last rays of the sun painting the horizon in hues of gold and orange. You can feel the soft grass beneath your bare feet, a gentle breeze caresses your skin, and the fresh scent of earth fills your nostrils.

Begin walking down the hill, each step deliberate, feeling the connection to the land. The sounds of the evening come to life around you – the distant call of a bird, the rustle of leaves, the whisper of the wind.

With every step, you grow more in tune with your senses. You can taste the cool air as it gently parts for your passage, sweet and tangy with a hint of the sea.

The hill slopes gently to a pebbled shore where a small boat awaits you, bobbing softly with the tide. You step into the boat and take the oars in your hands. With a strong pull, you move away from the land and into the realm of water and mist.

The sea is calm, the waves lull you into a deeper state of serenity. You row over the waves – one, two, three – each one taking you further from the mundane world, deeper into the Otherworld.

Four, five, six – each wave is larger than the last, a gentle giant lifting you up and setting you down again, cradled by the sea.

Seven, eight, nine – the ninth wave is the threshold, the liminal space between worlds. As you cross it, a dense fog surrounds you, and when it lifts, you find yourself approaching an enchanted island.

The shore of the island greets you with the soft murmur of a river. You follow the riverbank, guided by the luminous glow of fireflies dancing in the twilight.

Ahead, by the water's edge, you see her – the guardian goddess of this Otherworldly place. Her aura is one of powerful serenity, her eyes reflecting the wisdom of ages.

She beckons you closer and offers you a cup, carved from the finest wood, filled with water from the river that sparkles with its own inner light. As you drink, a profound peace fills you, a sense of wholeness and understanding.

The goddess speaks words of ancient truth, her voice a melody that resonates within your very soul. She offers guidance, comfort, and a message meant only for you. Listen with your heart, and you will understand.

With a heart full of gratitude, you bid farewell to the goddess and make your way back to the boat. You row back across the waters, the waves now carrying you gently back to the shore.

Take a deep breath in, feeling the energy return to your limbs. Wiggle your fingers and toes, feeling the earth's support beneath you. Whenever you feel ready, gently bring your awareness back to your surroundings

As you open your eyes, bring back with you the peace from the journey, the wisdom of the goddess, and the warmth of the light. Carry these gifts into your waking life, knowing you can return to this Otherworldly island whenever you seek the guidance of its guardian.

Part II

Working with Modron

Chapter 4

Modron and the Wheel of the Year

Before diving into specific aspects of Modron, this chapter will suggest ways in which her veneration can be included in the pagan Wheel of the Year, which is shared by neopagans of many different traditions as a way of honoring the turning of the seasons and associated festivals. It is a core aspect of many nature spiritualities, although it can be adapted to suit both the local environment and the practitioner.

Although what follows is based on how I personally honor Modron throughout the eightfold wheel, the concept of the Wheel of the Year revolving around a Mother Goddess who has a Divine Son is not new or exclusive to Celtic practice. In fact, an overarching myth of the Goddess and her son/lover God was at the heart of the original Wiccan Wheel of the Year, generally attributed in the form as we now know it by to Gerald Gardner, father of Wicca, and Ross Nichols, father of modern Druidry. While many of the festivals, such as Samhain, Yule etc., were known in different places in the ancient Western world, they were not all practiced together by any one people, and so this eightfold tradition is fundamentally neopagan.

Gardner drew on Classical agricultural myths, as well as the work of James Fraser in the *Golden Bough,* to formulate his Goddess and God myth, and there are also echoes of Osiris and Isis. The Mother gives birth to the Divine Child at Yule (showing similarities with Christian myth also) and becomes fertile as the land warms and the God grows. She is heavily pregnant by harvest time, at which point the God is sacrificed as an allegory of the reaping of the grain, to become Lord of the Underworld at Samhain.

As neopaganism and Wicca itself has grown and evolved, different traditions have used different myths and deities to symbolize the points on the Wheel of the Year, and among specifically Goddess worshippers, such as Dianic Wiccans, the Wheel has been conceptualized as allegorical to aspects of the Goddess without the God. For polytheists from a particular tradition such as Celtic, or working with a specific pantheon, different deities may be acknowledged at each festival. What follows then is based squarely in neopagan tradition, while incorporating my own devotion to Modron. Feel free to use, change, discard or be inspired by the following Wheel of the Year, as you wish.

Yule

Yule is the longest night of the year, and often associated with both the rebirth of the light and with the darkness of winter. Winter may be a time of rest and recuperation, of nourishment and warm comforting arms in the dark, or it may be a time of hopelessness, illness, grief or even depression. It may indeed feel like the Wasteland, where nothing grows and it feels as though the dark will never be over. Psychologically, we are in the Underworld. The Underworld may be a place of challenges, where we confront our fears. It may be a period of welcome hibernation. Whichever way it comes upon us, there is a time of waiting or wandering, of being unsure where the path ahead leads. Yet the Mother Goddess is with us even in the longest night; she both is the night itself and the Divine Spark, and however dark it may seem, this is the time when the Divine Child, the Mabon, and the light within us all, is born once again. At Yule we can both celebrate the Great Mother who watches over us all and the light that shines in the deepest recesses of the Underworld.

I ritualise Yule both individually and as a family. As a family we celebrate, as many do at this time of year, by decorating trees, lighting candles, feasting and giving gifts. I do acknowledge the feast day of Jesus, whose teachings remain an inspiration to me, but I also honor other great teachers and 'lights' at this time and encourage my children to think of someone they would like to light a candle to recognize – we have had a variety of 'lights in the darkness' from Peppa Pig to Malala!

On a more personal level, if circumstances permit, I keep vigil on the longest night, just as birth companions would sit up with a mother in labor, keeping a flame burning and spending the night in meditation, divination, poetry writing and ritual. Firstly, I bathe using the oils frankincense and myrrh, which seems appropriate, then prepare an altar before the fire. On the altar I typically have the vigil flame, some evergreen, my writing tools and a Modron figurine. I spend time in meditation, asking the Goddess for inspiration before picking up my writing tools and seeing what comes. I typically do a divination asking what gifts are coming for my family in the next year, and what I need to give away. I think about what lessons the Underworld has had to teach me this year; what abundance may yet come out of the darkness. As the first rays of dawn creep in, I anoint myself with the oils, thanking the Goddess for the gift of life, before blowing out the flame.

Although my wheel focuses on Modron rather than her son, at this festival, so often and for so long associated with the birth of a Divine Child, symbolizing the eventual return of the light, it is her role of mother of Mabon that is in focus, as this is a large part of her mythos and the two are often depicted together.

Questions to ask yourself:

- Who or what symbolizes the Divine Son or Child for you? How can you honor them?
- What wants to be born in your life? What gift is the Goddess offering to you?

- What does the concept of 'light in the darkness' mean to you? How can you ritualise that?
- How can you be a light in the darkness in your own community?

Imbolc/Candlemas/St. Bridget's Day

The land is still in the grip of winter in Britain and Ireland, yet we begin to see the signs of spring. The first snowdrops push their way through the often still frozen ground and the first buds are seen. The birds are beginning, slowly at first, to return. In spite of the cold, we sense the energy rising. And we hear the call of new life, new beginnings, new adventures, new creations or new rebellions.

The Call may come many times and in many different ways; a longing for what we cannot name, the pull towards a lover who speaks to our soul, a sudden inability to bear falsity and unethical behavior, a job or travel opportunity. It could be a death or a birth, an unexplained tragedy or a subtle triumph, and often the Call comes in unexpected ways. We may be scared, but we must answer it. Something that is both wild and wise within us calls back; 'Yes, yes. Finally, yes!' And we set off on the path. As the wheel turns slowly but inevitably towards high summer, we begin the work of bringing our deepest selves back to the light.

A festival of creativity and initiation, I will make a crown of evergreen and snowdrops for the altar, surrounded by white candles. If I have been pondering any new projects during the winter I will bless these with intention in ritual space and begin them shortly afterwards.

There is an association also at this time of year with milk, and although I don't typically drink dairy I will source local, free range and organic milk and use this both for cooking and a ritual drink, thanking the Goddess for the return of fertility to the land.

I also use this festival as a time to ask for healing of myself if necessary, loved ones, my community and the world, and usually ritualise these with a prayer and then an offering into the nearby stream. I also anoint myself with Chalice Well water from the holy well at Glastonbury, or with water from Madron Well, if I have access.

The Goddess many invoke at this time of year is Brigid, who is traditionally celebrated on this day – it is her feast. Brigid, known throughout the British Isles also as Brigit, Brid, Bride and Brigantia, is a goddess of poetry, fire, smithcraft, healing, war, fertility, the sun as well as the moon, and midwifery. Like Modron she has an aspect as a Triple Goddess, and has been Christianised into St Bridget. Bridget is known as a midwife (as Matrona may have been) and she is also associated with holy wells and in particular Brigid's Well at Kildare. Many pilgrims, both Christian and pagan, make their way there at Imbolc to hang clootie rags in the tree as petitions for healing. I have often felt that there is a link between Brigid and Modron, but this is a subjective feeling as I have found little to corroborate this and indeed, other aspects of their mythos are very different. Reliefs of Brigantia often look very similar to those of Matrona, however.

To venerate Modron herself at this time of year I see her in her role of nursing mother and midwife, as displayed on the Matrona and Matronae sculptures, This makes Imbolc a good time to do fertility and womb blessing rituals in her name, as well as Mother Blessings for pregnant women and people.

Questions to ask yourself:

- How are you being nurtured? How do you nurture others and yourself? Your community? Your land?

- What intentions do you wish to set for this year? What small action can you take to make a start on bringing them to actuality?
- Do you know any new mothers or parents? How could you reach out to offer your support?

Spring Equinox

Spring is here! Life has returned to the land, though the weather may still be wild, and the animals are beginning to frolic. The Bright Maiden has returned, and she blesses us with her abundance. In my wheel, this is the time of the drinking of the chalice – taking in the energies of the land and the goddess and the blessings that are on our way. We are now fully committed on our path, part of the spiral journey, part of the ever flowing and ever changing dance of life. At this point in our journey we may notice new talents coming to the fore or the resurgence of old talents, bursts of insight, new or reconciled relationships – or perhaps the ending and transforming of them. The sap is rising, and we drink the elixir of the Goddess.

To ritualise the Spring Equinox in my own life, this is typically a time of family fun and feasting. We often go camping at this time of year, weather permitting, and may build a fire and tell stories and share our wishes and dreams and that to which we wish to give life. I usually do a traditional egg hunt for the children, preferably using fresh eggs from the local free-range farm with the longed for chocolate egg at the end. I also do a 'spring clean' in the run up to the Equinox, of anything physical or emotional that has grown cobwebs! I typically have a burst of energy at this time of year but am also prone to colds and so will make echinacea, nettle and dandelion tea and steam baths which I can also use as a ritual bath and drink.

As a personal ritual I will place painted eggs, flowers and anything symbolizing the hare on the altar, and give thanks for my blessings as well as asking for release from anything that needs to be let go of. I will often be working on a creative project so I may say a prayer for continued inspiration, as well as planting seedlings to symbolize my projects coming to fruition.

At this time, Modron is coming into her aspect as a fertility goddess, and it is a good time for fertility rituals and to honor her life-giving element and association with water. The story of Modron and Urien can be ritualized and performed, and she can be thanked for the returning fertility of the land. She is the Maiden sometimes shown in sculptures of the Matronae. You also might like to perform chalice rituals or rituals with water – it is often still raining a lot in the Northern hemisphere, and so if you have a local river or stream, it is likely to be full and flowing!

Questions to ask yourself:

- What does the Maiden aspect of the Goddess signify to you? Does she resonate? Why or why not?
- What is becoming fertile in your own life?
- Think about the motif of drinking from the Chalice or the river. What does this signify to you, and how can you ritualise it?

Beltane/May Day/Brightening

It is May. Early summer, the air smells of blossom and the land is fertile. This is traditionally a time of year for lovers, echoing the energy of the earth as bees pollinate, animals are in season and the flowers bloom. Having drunk from the Chalice it is time to set off down the path of the Beloved, which may manifest as entering a new relationship with a lover but is just as likely to be a new relationship with the Divine or our own sweet selves. If we stay true on the path, this will lead us towards our wild soul, but there are distractions aplenty and it is easy to get waylaid with things – and people – that are shiny but have no substance. Much as at this time of year, as legend has it, people would become enchanted by the Faeryworld, often staying overlong and finding their lifeforce sapped.

Modron, however, is the giver of the life force, and this is another perfect time of year to ritualise the coming together of Modron and Urien, and the subsequent birth of twins, who are both blessed. Urien is the only one brave enough to risk the barking dogs (likely associated with the legendary Hounds of Annwn) and win her love.

Others read this myth differently, however, and suggest that, as in many other myths of this type, especially those containing Otherworldly women and water elements, Urien rapes and/or kidnaps Modron. This would be potentially a Wasteland myth and indeed, although in his legends Urien initially becomes a great King, this goes before a significant fall. For those struggling to recover from sexual assault of any kind, these myths have particular resonance, and Beltane is a good time of year to focus on individual sexual healing.

Personally, however, as Modron blesses Urien and happily goes to him with the twins a year later, I do not feel this is a rape myth. Her hounds cease barking and become quiet for Urien, suggesting that he is indeed the lover she has been waiting for. This suggests to me a fertility and Sovereignty myth, in which the worthy ruler marries the Goddess of the land, rather than a Wasteland myth similar to that which we encountered in Chapter 2. Although Modron appears to have been cursed to wash at the river until Urien – a 'Christian king' – arrives, this is likely to be a Christian gloss on a much older myth, one perhaps designed to bring together pagan and Christian elements and add authority to Urien's reign.

Fertility and sex magic are ideal for Beltane, and if you are single you may wish to visit Madron Well or a similar site and ask for a vision of your future partner, much as An Katty described the maidens of Madron doing in May!

Questions to ask yourself:

- How do I celebrate and integrate my sexuality? Have I been wounded in this area and if so, what do I need to heal? How can the Goddess help me do this?
- If I have an intimate relationship, how can I celebrate this?

Midsummer

The Summer Solstice is the high point of the solar year; when the days are longest and the land warm and fertile. The Goddess steps fully into the light and into her own sovereignty and her own queenship. For some of us, at different times of life a sense of personal sovereignty may include an external achievement such as career success or a relationship transition such as marriage or parenthood, but the fullest expression of this phase is inner fulfillment, which may or may not be marked by an outer change, but which brings a deep inner shift. Regardless of what travails life has in store, once someone has stepped into their true inner sovereignty, it will always be theirs for the claiming.

To ritualise Midsummer I often create a solar mandala in the garden with the children and share a noonday picnic. I may also tend a flame in the firepit and use this as the basis for ritual, although typically for me Midsummer is not a time for formal ritual but for family, fun and celebration.

I venerate Modron on my altar as the Celtic Great Mother, associating her with the abundance of the land and the flow of river water – I put a picture of the river Marne on my altar, fruit and flowers.

Questions to ask yourself:

- What have been the highpoints of your life? How can you celebrate and express gratitude for these? What do you wish to give thanks for?
- It is the holiday season; can you take a day off, purely to have fun and enjoy yourself? Revel in the gifts of the Goddess.

Lammas/Lughnasadh/Dimming

Summer is at its height, and the days are warm and lazy – or possibly muggy and stormy – yet the nights are growing longer again and the Wheel of the Year is once again turning. This is the time of early harvest, the first fruits and the baking of bread, a time for gratitude and abundance and a festival that we can associate particularly with Matrona and the Matronae with their arms full of grain, fruit baskets and overflowing cornucopias. It is also a time of restoration and justice, of giving back – of restoring the balance.

Lughnasadh for me is a time to give thanks and to give offerings. Bread is baked, and the first piece given back to the Earth – the Goddess. Last year, I also offered myself back to the Goddess, a rededication to her as Modron, and made an offering at the Red and White Springs in Glastonbury, a place that has much spiritual meaning for me. I also offered time to serve at the Goddess Temple there.

Questions to ask yourself:

- At this time of harvest, what can you give back? What 'first fruits' can you offer?
- Is your 'basket' full? If not, why not? What do you need, and who can you ask for help?

Autumn Equinox

At the Autumn Equinox the year is in balance once more – and then turns towards the dark. This is the time of the Dark Goddess, She Who Returns. It is a time of turning inward after the action and plentifulness of summer, a time to rest, reflect, and learn.

The Equinox is also a harvest festival, and at this time of year churches are often doing extra collections for local Food Banks, as do other religious communities, including some neopagans. I often take stock on a personal level, looking at what in my life needs to let go of and what needs to be shored up. It is a time for personal inventory, thanksgiving – and for turning inwards. On my altar will be fruit and vegetables, especially apples. This is a good time for guided journeying to the Otherworld.

There is often some confusion over the name of this festival. Although all of the festivals have different cultural names, you may see the Autumn Equinox called 'Mabon,' which might seem perfect for the theme of this book. However, as far as we know there is no pre-modern link between Mabon/Maponus as a Celtic deity and the Autumn Equinox – in fact, the Celts do not seem to have celebrated the Autumn Equinox at all. It was given the name by Aidan Kelly in the 1970s, in reference to Mabon as a son of the Mother Goddess. However, as far as we know, Mabon/Maponus was not a dying and rising god who became Lord of the Underworld; there is no known suggestion that this is part of his mythos. The only hint of a possibility – and it is tenuous – is that on the *Tablet of Chamalieres*, a Gaulish prayer tablet excavated in 1971, an inscription to Maponus reads 'quicken us by the magic of the underworld spirits,' which might mean he was at some point seen as a deity who could mediate between mortals and the Underworld.

If you we accept Gruffydd's thesis that the story of Modron and Mabon has links with Classical myths of the coming of winter, then we could use this festival to remember or ritualise the imprisonment and exile of Mabon and the grief of Modron, as a tale that is allegorical of the end of summer and the coming Wasteland of winter. Be aware, though, that this is a modern linking.

I do personally see Modron at this time of year as both Mother of the Harvest and the Grieving Mother, and this is a good time of year for rituals involving loss, especially pregnancy and baby loss. I will explore this theme further in the next chapter. Also, however, I turn again to the Washer at the Ford and Sovereignty myths and look at the darker aspects of these. Although in Modron's tale she brings life and fertility rather than death and, as discussed above, there is no intimation that Urien raped her, many similar myths do involve a rape, and either the land becomes barren or the goddess/otherworldly woman herself is in exile. Reading stories of selkies, mermaids and the French goddess Melusine as well as the Elucidation will give you a wider understanding of these myths and help you to explore them and their meanings for yourself.

In keeping with this theme, as well as honoring Modron at this time of year I also acknowledge the Irish Goddess Aine, a Faery Queen who is also a dark goddess in her lesser known guise as selkie or mermaid. A newer myth has her being captured by an Irish Earl, who steals her cloak while she was bathing in a river. She gains her freedom and returns to her lake in County Limerick; a myth which has led to suggestion she has associations with the Lady of the Lake, therefore subtly linking her with Modron.

Questions to ask yourself:

- How can you help others who have less than you to prepare for the winter?

- What have you lost this year? What do the themes of exile and return mean to you?

Samhain/Halloween/Hallows

Winter has arrived, and this is a time for turning inward and reflection and seeking inner wisdom. It is also a time of taking stock of the year that has passed and of honoring the ancestors and loved ones that have died this year. This time of year is ruled by the Wise Woman or Crone and she often appears in one's life as a teacher or guide through the ensuing winter, or time in the Underworld. She may appear in the external world or one's psyche or both, and helps us to integrate and channel our inner resources. We move into a new level of knowing and seeing.

As I am of Irish (and Welsh Kale) ethnicity, Samhain is an important festival for me. The children may join in with more commercial festivals of Halloween, but for me this is a time to journey inwards and commune with the ancestors and the beloved dead, and hold grief and gratitude rituals for those I have lost this year. I may write a guided meditation for this process or attend a ritual with this purpose in mind, or I lay a place at the table for family members who have passed and build an ancestral altar. I may also build or walk a labyrinth, and generally practice divination.

The goddess who rules this festival for many is the Morrigan in her guise of Witch-Queen and Crone. The Morrigan is the Wise One, the Wisdom Keeper, the Phantom Queen and Lady of the Dead. As discussed above, she has been linked with Modron, and this is a time to consider that Modron has a darker aspect, as at the Autumn Equinox. Remembering the statues of Matronae with snakes, I will have a representation of a serpent or snake on my altar, as well as apples to symbolize, not harvest this time, but journeying to the Otherworld. On my ancestral altar, to honor Modron as mother, I pay particular attention to my maternal ancestors, and to my grandmothers.

Questions to ask yourself:

- Who are your maternal ancestors? How can you acknowledge them? We will explore this further in the next chapter.
- What resonance does the symbol of the snake have for you? Do you fear it? Why?
- What are your feelings around death and mortality?

As well as the Wheel of the Year, most neopagans take notice of the phase of the moon and include this in ritual or magical practice. While Modron is not explicitly associated with the moon, she is with water and motherhood, often seen as primary moon correspondences. You may like to think about what moon phases you would find it appropriate to work with Modron on; for me it is Full Moon, Waning Gibbous and Dark Moon, as I feel these correspond with her aspects as Mother, the late summer harvest, and the Mother of the Light in the Darkness.

Chapter 5

The Ancestral Mother

This chapter will focus on Modron's role as mother; firstly in a very human way as we look at her twin faces of fertility and loss, and secondly as she relates to the concept of an ancestral Great Mother.

Fertility

Named explicitly as a mother, having outdoor sex with kings near fords – resulting in twins – and with her Gallic-Roman precursor associated with babies, fruit and overflowing cornucopias, Modron's role as a fertility goddess seems clear. As Simek suggests, she may also have been called upon as a divine midwife, a protector in childbirth at a time when maternal mortality would have been high. Fruit and grain show her as intimately connected with the fertility of the land, and her association with healing waters and holy wells make it likely that some of the votive offerings to her were requests for pregnancies and healthy babies.

Her well at Madron, at least according to An Katty who we met earlier, was regularly used by maidens looking for husbands – and following that, babies. She is an ideal goddess for use in fertility rituals, and I have provided a suggested ritual outline below which you may wish to try. Of course, if you are struggling to get pregnant, please consult your doctor first and foremost. There is no reason, however, why you cannot use ritual alongside fertility treatment. It could also be adapted for those who are adopting via a surrogate, or for any non-pregnancy creative endeavor which you wish to ripen.

For the ritual, choose a time which is meaningful to you. This could be a full moon night to harness the energy of completion and abundance, or during Beltane (May Day), which is traditionally a festival of fertility. Or, if you are trying to get pregnant and tracking your menstrual cycle, try it at ovulation! Find a quiet and comfortable space where you won't be disturbed. Ideally, this would be outdoors, in a garden or natural setting, to connect with the earth's energy. If you can find a place near water, or a hawthorn tree, then better. Hawthorn has long been used in fertility rites, and hawthorn trees surround Madron Well. Set up a small altar with a representation of the goddess as Matrona, which could be a statue or an image. Include symbols of fertility, such as eggs, seeds, a bowl of earth, a small pot of honey, and a chalice of water. You might also include a green or orange candle to represent life and fertility.

Begin by cleansing yourself and the ritual space. You can do this by smudging with sage or asperging with salt water to purify the area and create a sacred space. Stand in the center of your space and visualize a circle of protective energy around you, moving clockwise. As you do this, say:

> *"I cast this circle to create a sacred space, no negative energy may enter this place"*

Light the candle on your altar, and then say:

> *"Great goddess Matrona, Divine Mother, whose waters of life bring forth the spring, I call upon you. Grace this sacred space with your presence, and bless this rite of fertility."*

Place your offerings on the altar, saying:

> *"I offer these gifts to Matrona, with love and with a hopeful heart."*

Take the seeds and plant them in the bowl of earth, symbolizing the planting of your intentions. As you do this, visualize your wish for fertility, whether it be physical, as in a child, or metaphorical, as in the fertility of a project or new endeavor. Pour the honey over the seeds, saying:

> *"As honey sweetens life, so may my life be sweetened with the fruit of my intentions."*

Raise the chalice of water, and pour some over the seeds, saying:

> *"As water nurtures the earth, so may I be nurtured and so may my intentions grow strong and healthy."*

Sit quietly and meditate on your intentions. Imagine the goddess Matrona blessing you with fertility and abundance. Feel her nurturing energy as a warm, glowing light that surrounds you

When you are ready, thank the goddess for her presence and blessings:

> *"Thank you, Matrona, for your blessings. May the seeds of my intentions blossom, and may you always be honored through the bounty of life."*

Visualize the circle of energy dissipating and returning to the earth, saying:

> *"The circle is open, but unbroken, may the peace of the goddess be ever in my heart."*

After the ritual is complete, eat and drink to ground yourself. This is also a way to share in the offerings you made to the goddess. And, of course, an excellent post-ritual activity, especially if you are trying for a baby, is to make love.

Remember to approach the ritual with respect and sincerity, and always close with gratitude. The power of such rituals often lies in the intention and energy you bring to them, so focus on the qualities you wish to draw into your life.

Loss

The flip side to the fertile, abundant Matrona with her nursing breasts and overflowing cornucopias is the grieving Modron, and adjacent to her Rhiannon and Branwen, whose babies have been taken from them. Perhaps this motif does relate to an older seasonal myth similar to that of Demeter, but from a sociological analysis it speaks to something much more human. This association of motherhood with loss would have been a powerful one in a time where women were encouraged to be mothers above all else, yet infant mortality was high, pregnancy and especially childbirth could be dangerous, and miscarriage and stillbirth were poorly understood. For pagans today, a goddess who grieves with us can be a comfort and a potent way to ritualise and process our grief after baby loss.

Creating a ritual to help with grieving and processing the profound loss of a baby is a delicate and personal process. This ritual is intended to provide comfort and a means to connect with Modron's compassionate and nurturing energy during such a difficult time, and can be performed alone or with others.

Choose a quiet time when you are unlikely to be disturbed, possibly during dusk or dawn, which are times of transition. Find a peaceful area where you feel safe and comfortable, indoors or outdoors. You may want to have a small table or area to set up a symbolic altar. Place items on the altar that remind you of your baby. This may include a scan picture, a blanket, or a piece of clothing. Include also an image or symbol of Modron, a candle (perhaps blue to represent healing or white for peace), a bowl of water, and a few pieces of sea glass or stones to represent your journey and the permanence of your love.

Begin by cleansing yourself and the space. You might want to take a warm bath before you start, or you could use sage or incense to purify the area around your altar.

Sit or stand before your altar and take several deep breaths. Visualize a comforting light surrounding you, creating a protective sphere. When you feel ready, say:

> *"I cast this circle to create a sacred space, a haven for my heart and my memories."*

Light the candle, focusing on its flame. When you feel centered, say:

> *"Goddess Modron, Great Mother, you who understand the deepest of loves and the sharpest of losses, I call upon you.*
> *Please join me and lend me your strength and comfort."*

Hold the item that reminds you of your baby, and speak to them. Share your memories, your love, and your dreams for them. Allow yourself to feel whatever emotions arise, knowing this space is held for you and your baby.

Take a bowl of water and the sea glass or stones. One by one, drop them into the water, each representing a wish, a dream, a memory, a sorrow. As each stone touches the water, visualize your emotions being acknowledged by Modron. Say:

> *"Just as stones are shaped by the sea, so too are our lives shaped by love and loss. May the waters of healing flow over my heart."*

Sit quietly with the presence of the goddess. You may feel her as a comforting presence, a warm embrace, or a sense of not being alone. Ask Modron for her guidance in navigating your grief, for her strength to carry you through the coming days.

When you are ready, thank the goddess for her presence, saying:

"Thank you, Modron, for your comfort and compassion. May I carry your strength with me as I walk this path of healing."

Extinguish the candle, saying:

"Though the flame is extinguished, the warmth remains. Though the circle is opened, the love endures."

In the days and weeks that follow, allow yourself to return to the feelings and messages of this ritual whenever you need to. Consider keeping a journal of your thoughts and experiences as you continue to process your grief.

The Ancestral Motherline

The ancestral mother to the Brythonic pantheon of gods was Don (known as Danu to the Irish). It is tempting, given the auditory similarities in their names, to link her directly to Modron, but Don/Danu is associated with the river Danube, and Modron/Matrona with the river Marne. It is more likely that they emerged entirely separately as local and tribal deities, before their worship grew and spread and they became part of the same 'family tree'.

In the Welsh stories that we have discussed, Modron has become a distinct persona with her own family history, presented to us as the daughter of Afallach. Afallach is described elsewhere as the son of the god Beli, and while no mother is mentioned, Beli is generally linked with Don. This would make Modron, mother of the human Owain, the granddaughter of Don.

However, we know that, in her earlier guise as Matrona, evidence for her worship is far older than the tales as they are recorded in the *Mabinogi* and the *Triads*, and there are a few more facts to consider which, while far from definite proof of anything, are certainly interesting and pose further questions.

The constellation known as Cassiopeia looks somewhat like a throne and was often depicted as such in the Classical world, with various sculptures of goddesses being shown depicted on a similarly shaped throne, often while nursing a baby (Cassiopeia is situated within the Milky Way, sometimes viewed as the milk of a goddess to the Greeks). Similar sculptures are found dedicated to the Egyptian goddess Isis – and to the Celtic goddess Matrona.

Viewed from a side angle, Cassiopeia makes a distinctive 'W' shape which is sometimes seen as breasts, and this can also be seen on various goddess sculptures, including on some of the Matronaes. (Dashu, 2017)

Cassiopeia was known by the Brythonic Celts as Llys Don, or 'the place of Don.' This indicates, given the details on the sculptures mentioned above, that Modron may indeed at some point, have been considered as an aspect of Don/Danu, the ancestral mother of the Celts.

Given that Matrona/Modron is a title as much as a name, we can speculate as to what extent she was cognate with other Celtic goddesses and whether she can be viewed as an overarching Mother Goddess.

As an ancestral mother, it may be that Modron carries more meaning in her mythos and symbols than that which originated in Indo-European cultures such as the peoples we refer to in modern times as 'the Celts.' Matrona's reliefs and sculptures show her as identified with agriculture and the harvest, associated by some with the Greek goddess Demeter. While Gruffydd believed this pointed at a Proto-Indo-European myth, it is more likely that these goddess associations predate this, belonging instead to the Neolithic farming communities that Proto-Indo-European tribes – nomadic and warlike pastoralists – gradually took over, sometimes by violence, sometimes by integration, most often a mixture of both. These new integrated cultures not only brought new gods but often absorbed older gods, or aspects of them, into their pantheons. In the Greek pantheon, it is believed that Demeter and Dionysius were carried over from Neolithic farming culture. If this is true of Demeter it may also be true of 'Dea Matrona' who shares so many of her symbols. In the next chapter we will see how aspects of her as a river goddess may be even more ancient. While her son Maponus became syncretised with Apollo, as Mabon he has attributes that suggest motifs that we see as far back as the shamanic Paleolithic – his association with hunting and beasts. It may be that these even older motifs came into the Mabon stories via local sources, or that Maponus did have these associations before he became syncretised into the Greco-Roman pantheon; we simply don't know. But we do know that Modron has very old roots.

This is also suggested by Mabon himself. While patriarchal and certainly warlike in many ways, many tribes of the Celts were notably matrilineal, tracing ancestry through the mother, rather than the father, and afforded women significant rights (at least, elite women) compared to the Greeks and Romans. It has been suggested that this matrilineal feature was adopted from the earlier Neolithic communities and matrilineality has been associated with more egalitarian and less warlike societies. (Dashu,2017) The very title Mabon ap Modron illustrates this – we are never told who Mabon's father is, in fact this seems to be completely unimportant. What is worth noting about his lineage is his Motherline. This is significant because by the time the tales of the *Mabinogi* were recorded, society was becoming ever more patriarchal and women and gendered others losing ever more rights – including the rights of mothers to guardianship over their own children. This gives us another hint that the tale of Mabon and Modron is far older than the point at which it was written down.

So, what can the idea of Modron as an ancestral mother offer us today? Mother goddesses have long been seen as important by feminist theologians, as evidence both that God was not always an authoritarian father, and as offering a view of women's role as mothers not as a curse from the Garden of Eden but as a sacred and divine function. If goddesses are mothers, then mothers, some argue, are akin to goddesses. Others, including some in the neopagan community, have criticized the idea of a Great Mother Goddess as unhelpful and essentialist, arguing that, while our ability to bear life and nurture life are sacred, so are our many other abilities. Women are not just breasts and wombs and vaginas – and we do not all experience those things in the same way. If motherhood is sacred it is as much because *we all have mothers* as because some of us can be or choose to be. For this reason the modern conception of Goddess as Maiden, Mother and Crone is seen as potentially problematic as it is so intimately tied up in reproductive cycles and does not apply to so many women – particularly in an age where we live longer and there are many stages between motherhood and menopause. It has also been used too many times to exclude trans women, who have their own unique relationship to the Divine through their bodies – in fact this begs the question of whether there is not a particularly potent form of sacrality in the fluidity and intertwining of masculine and feminine aspects.

While these criticisms are valid, and I tend to agree, I believe we can venerate mother goddesses without denying other aspects of Deity or the diversity of her worshippers. Celtic deities themselves are diverse, with goddesses as likely to be warlike and dark as much as they are benevolent life-givers.

One way in which I work with Modron as a mother goddess is by honoring my ancestral lineage, which is predominantly

Celtic, and particularly my maternal ancestors, or Motherline. Ancestor work tends to be popular among pagans, and deities which represent our ancestral lineage can help us greatly with this. Whether you are male, female or non-binary, trans, cis or genderfluid, connecting with your Motherline (or whatever you choose to name it) can be powerful magic.

Our Motherlines are often all too blocked by trauma stretching back over the last few thousand years of a patriarchal, dominating society. Recent breakthroughs in epigenetics suggest that trauma may be both stored in our bodies and passed down through the generations. We may literally carry the wounds of our foremothers in our mitochondrial DNA.

Yet we also, spiritually or otherwise, carry their wisdom. And surely if our very cells can in some strange way remember the long slow torture of millennia of oppression they also remember a time when it was not this way? When we lived in greater harmony with nature and each other? And we can pass that on too to our descendants, both physical, spiritual and those we influence in our everyday lives. I believe our Motherline has much to teach us, and it was only when I started working with Modron that I was able to more easily access this ancestral wisdom.

To begin working with your Motherline, you can start close, with your own grandmothers, tracing their stories back and perhaps using this as the beginning of family tree work, discovering where your ancestors lived and worked. Or you can start back in the distant past by researching what is known about the prehistory of your ancestral locations. Once you have some information about your ancestors to work with, represent them on your altar, if you have one, or build an altar specifically for their veneration, perhaps temporarily such as for Samhain, or more permanently. Place on it items that represent them or their places. You might use photographs for more recent ancestors, or sculptures, fabrics, stones, pictures of cave paintings or artifacts for your ancestors back in prehistory. I find Venus of Willendorf figurines a good choice for representing Palaeolithic female-bodied ancestors.

Guided Journey to Meet Your Motherline

Settle into a space where you feel comfortable and safe. Allow your eyes to gently close as you draw in a slow, deep breath. As you breathe out, envision a comforting, radiant light – a light filled with the warmth of the sun's last rays – beginning to caress the crown of your head.

Feel this light as a presence of pure relaxation, traveling across your body, starting from your head, flowing downward. It soothes your brow, eases your eyelids, and brings stillness to your inner gaze.

As you inhale again, this serene light glides over your face, relaxing your cheeks and unclenching your jaw. It continues, descending, wrapping your throat in warmth, releasing any held words or tension.

The light, imbued with a sense of tranquility, pours over your shoulders, a golden river smoothing away any burdens, leaving your muscles loose and free.

It sweeps down your arms, to your elbows, wrists, and finally your hands, filling the spaces between your fingers with a gentle glow.

Your chest and back bask in this light, each breath deeper, more restful than the last, as if the light itself is breathing with you.

The glow moves to encircle your abdomen and lower back, a comforting weight that untangles the knots within, allowing your innermost self to soften.

It descends further still, through your hips, along your thighs, a cascade of peace that takes with it all the heaviness of the day.

Your knees, calves, and ankles all succumb to this peaceful progression, and by the time the light reaches your feet, you are completely embraced by relaxation.

With your body completely at rest, imagine you stand atop a gentle slope, the sky painted with the dusky colors of twilight. The air is cool and sweet, filled with the scent of wildflowers and grass. Each step you take down the hillside is a step deeper into calm, the soft earth beneath you a testament to the timelessness of the land.

At the hill's base lies a serene shoreline, where a single, wooden boat rocks slightly with the whispering tide. You step into this vessel, taking the oars, feeling their rough grain beneath your hands.

Rowing across the misty sea, you are lulled by the gentle rhythm of the waves. With each set of nine waves that you crest you sense that you are not only traversing water, but also time itself.

The mist clears, revealing the welcoming sight of an island, suspended in a sea of stars that are reflected upon the water's surface. You reach the island and get out, stepping onto soft grass. A tributary from the sea flows into a river, which seems to sing as it flows. When you enter, you walk to its banks.

Here, the river calls you to walk alongside it, and as you follow its course, you find yourself walking backwards in time with each step.

Ancient trees line the river, their leaves whispering secrets of old, and the stars above mirror those within the water, guiding you on your path backward through the centuries.

The river leads you to a cavern entrance, an ancient womb of the earth. As you enter, the cool, damp air greets you, and you start to walk down, down a stone spiral staircase within the darkness of the cave. The walls seem to shine with a dim light from within, giving you just enough light to see your way.

You step down the last stair and reach the heart of this hallowed space. A fire is burning, casting shadows across the walls of the cave. An old woman, regal and queenly, sits on a rocky throne before the fire. She is the ancestral goddess, whose gaze fixes you with the eternity of your lineage. She is the embodiment of your maternal ancestors, her presence a tapestry woven with their lives and experiences.

You approach her and she reaches out, her touch a bridge to your past. With words that resonate deep within your bones, she imparts to you the collective wisdom of your foremothers. Their voices, their laughter, their sorrows, and their triumphs are shared with you through her. Listen, for these echoes form the foundation upon which you stand.

With her blessings, you will carry the wisdom of generations back to the surface. You bid her goodbye and return up the stone steps. Exiting the cave, you trace your path back along the river, the stars fading as dawn's light begins to touch the horizon of this ancient world.

You embark once more on the boat, each stroke of the oars carrying you forward through time, returning you to the shore at the base of the hill.

The warm light returns to guide you up the hill. With every upward step, the mist of the Otherworld dissolves, and the sense of your own world becomes sharper.

The light coalesces around you, a cocoon of warmth, as you begin to feel the gentle weight of your own body once more. Your breath deepens, your fingers and toes start to move, and when you're ready, you can open your eyes.

Chapter 6

The Chalice of Modron

Our ancestors, from the Paleolithic to the Iron Age, appear to have regarded water as sacred, hardly surprising given that an abundant water source would have been essential for a community to flourish and indeed, for its very survival. From the Bronze Age onwards, people increasingly settled along rivers or near lakes and bogs. Water was associated with the Otherworld by the Celts, perhaps because water would have seemed to have a mysterious origin; miraculously gushing forth from the ground. (Beck, 2015)

As we moved into the modern world, water continued to have a symbolic and magical aspect. It is one of the four elements in magical traditions and one of the three realms of Land, Sea and Sky in the Celtic tradition. It is typically associated with healing, serpents, the West and the Feminine.

As we saw in the first part of this book, Modron/Matrona was associated with water, with both rivers, fords and wellsprings, and votive offerings to her were found across Gaul at springs believed to have curative properties. A meaningful way to connect with her in the present age is through her aspect as a water goddess.

A water ritual for healing can be a serene and transformative practice. For this ritual, using a chalice and natural spring or mineral water is a way to connect with the element of water's healing properties as well as Modron and her symbols.

Tools:

- A bowl or chalice that you find beautiful or meaningful
- Natural spring or mineral water

- A blue candle
- Crystals such as aquamarine, turquoise or blue lace agate
- A piece of cloth or ribbon in blue or silver

Set up your space in a way that feels clean, open, and comforting. Place your chalice in the center of your altar space. Arrange any crystals you are using around it and lay the cloth or ribbon in front of it. Begin by cleansing yourself and your space. If it's part of your practice, you can cast a circle to create a sacred and protected space, perhaps using the mineral water.

Hold your hands over the chalice of water and call upon the healing energies. You might say:

> *"Modron, keeper of the waters of life, I invoke your presence. May your cleansing power flow through me."*

Take a moment to hold the chalice with both hands and visualize a bright light – perhaps a gentle blue or shimmering silver – pouring from your hands into the water, infusing it with healing energy. If you have chosen to use crystals, place them gently in the water (ensure they are water-safe) to charge it with their properties. Sit comfortably and take a few deep breaths. As you hold the chalice, meditate on the water's ability to heal and cleanse. Visualize the water glowing with the healing light.

If you wish, you can now gently pour the water over your hands, feeling its cool touch and envisioning any physical or emotional pain being washed away. Then slowly sip the water, imagining its healing properties flowing through your body, reaching every cell, and restoring your well-being.

When you feel full of the water's healing energy, say a statement of gratitude and closure such as:

> *"Thank you, Modron of the healing waters, for your gentle strength. May this healing be sustained within me."*

Extinguish the candle, affirming the continuation of your healing process even as the light fades.

If any water remains, you can offer it to a plant as a way to pass on the healing energy to the earth.

Healing is a process, and it is important to nurture yourself following a healing ritual. Pay attention to your dreams, emotions, and physical sensations in the days that follow. Healing rituals can initiate a period of release and change, so be gentle with yourself as you process this experience.

The River Goddess

As well as her original association with the River Marne, there are various river names in France and across what were Gaulish territories which are derived from the name 'Matrona,' including the La Moder. Beck (2015) believes that, rather than all being dedicated to the same goddess persona, Gaul had a tradition of 'mother-rivers' which can be found in other Indo-European traditions. The Vedic *Rig Veda* gives rivers the epithet 'matritamas' or 'the mothers par excellence.' In the Iranian *Avesta,* they are the 'mataro gitayo' or 'living mothers.' The Avesta also mentions a mother goddess figure called Aravadi Sura Anahita, and describes her as 'life increasing and holy…who sends down …a flow of motherly waters…that run along the earth.' She is shown on a relief as bestowing a flower garland around the neck of a king, suggestive of a Sovereignty function.

As well as being associated with life and healing, rivers were also associated with funerary rites. Coffin boats have been found in rivers across Gaul, including in the Marne, where a five meter oak pirogue, or 'tomb-boat' was discovered, containing a human skeleton and weapons that indicate the deceased was an esteemed warrior or king.

Serpents – such as those depicted on some reliefs of the Matronae – were commonly associated with river goddesses, which seems to make sense when we consider that serpents were associated, in some of humanity's oldest myths and rituals (Coulson et al 2016) with life-giving water and healing. Only later were serpents widely demonized and seen as symbolic of evil.

It may be that the serpents came before the river goddesses, as our ancestors, particularly in the Paleolithic, were animistic, assigning spirits to natural phenomena such as trees, mountains and rivers. When they started to give images to these spirits, they were often animals before they took human form. River goddesses tended to be local tribal deities before their worship grew and spread, and are likely to have originally been what we now call 'genius loci', or 'spirits of place'. We will look at these more in the next chapter.

River rituals, or simply spending time near one, are an ideal way to connect with the energies of Modron, and a simple river ritual can be a powerful way to physically and symbolically release stress and worry. Rivers, with their flowing nature, are often associated with the movement of time and the release of energy. Here is a simple ritual outline you might find helpful, that is also great to do with children.

Find some natural biodegradable materials to represent your worries (e.g., leaves, twigs, flower petals, or small paper made from natural fibers). You will also need a pen that uses non-toxic, biodegradable ink if you wish to write down your worries.

Travel to a local river where you can safely access the water. As you walk, try to maintain a mindful state, noticing the environment around you, the sounds of nature, and the rhythm of your own footsteps.

Stand, sit, or kneel at the edge of the river, wherever you feel most comfortable and stable.

Hold the biodegradable material in your hands and close your eyes. Take several deep breaths, each time imagining your stress and worry flowing from your body into the items you are holding. You may also like to write or draw your stresses onto the material.

Open your eyes and one by one, place your items into the river. As each one begins to float away, visualize your stress and worries being carried away by the water. You may want to say a simple affirmation or chant as you do this, for example:

"River flow, take my stress, carry my worries, leave me refreshed."

After you have released all your items into the river, take a moment to feel the earth beneath your feet. Imagine roots extending from the soles of your feet down into the ground, anchoring you and drawing up a sense of calm and strength from the earth. Thank the river for helping you in this ritual of release.

River and water goddesses were also often seen in Sovereignty myths as we have discussed, where they may also represent the goddess of the land, who offers a drink of her life-giving water to the chosen king. The king, in order to keep her approval and his right to rule, must in turn guard and protect the land. In Sharon Blackie's adapted story from the *Elucidation*, discussed in Chapter 2, when the king does not uphold his end of the bargain – or violates the goddess – the water runs dry and the land becomes the Wasteland. We will look at this idea, and what relevance it has for the present age, in the next chapter.

Chapter 7

Guarding the Land

Sovereignty goddesses are a common theme in Celtic myth, and as we saw with the description of the goddess garlanding the king in the Persian *Avesta*, may be part of a Proto-Indo-European motif. Some have read it as symbolizing the merging of two cultures; the Neolithic farming communities with the nomadic invaders from the East. The goddess as Sovereignty then becomes absorbed into the new mythical cycle just as Demeter and Dionysius became part of the Greek Olympian pantheon.

But as we move into modern times, we can examine how any myth remains relevant for us today. This is how our practice remains fresh, and how we engage with myth and ritual as living things, not just ancient stories to be studied and then put aside. As a Sovereignty figure, one that symbolizes the fertility of the land and its life-giving waters, Modron charges us with its stewardship just as she did the kings of old.

And, collectively, we have failed. Certainly, our leaders and elites have done so – and often continue to. The Sovereignty tales and the story of the rape of the well maidens ensuing in the Wasteland is remarkably prescient when we consider the current climate crisis, and so Modron can be an ideal goddess to call upon when we are attempting to combat these things.

Nature spirituality, of which neopaganism is a part, may have a crucial role to play in tackling the current climate emergency by helping to restore our relationship to the land, a relationship which Modron symbolizes, especially in her oldest form as local river goddess or spirit. Our ancestors, as well as many indigenous peoples today, were animists before they were worshiping anthropomorphic deities, believing that each living thing, from animal to plant, had its own spirit. Ecosystems such as rivers, mountains and forests were also seen as living beings with their own spirit. Many nature spiritualities today aim to recapture this sense of animism and bring it back to our consciousness.

Animism – the idea that everything is ensouled – may also lead to a sense of pantheism, which at its simplest is the notion that the natural world as a whole is Divine. The Goddess, or whatever name we wish to give it, is the air we breathe, the water we drink, the lifegiving powers conception and birth, the dark matter that holds the Universe together, the mysterious dark energy that flows through all, the fiery energy of the Sun, the firing neurons of inspiration, orgasm, the blooming of flowers, the pulse of life within the Earth.

Pantheism argues for an all-inclusive Unity that pervades all things and yet is somehow more than the sum of its parts. As well as groundedness, there is Mystery here too, for our perceptions are limited to a certain manifestation of time and space. The challenge then is to hold the awareness of Mystery without the need to plunder it as we have done to the natural world, or describe it as some transcendent Other. As soon as we do so, we lose our sense of connection to the All, to the knowledge that we are an indivisible part of Nature, of the Divine, of the Creative Cosmos. We create a polarizing duality; light and dark, man and woman, black and white, good and evil.

In practice, this sense of nature as divine and of interconnection with all of life can provide a grounding for both our spiritual practice and our ethics. This may manifest in different ways depending on our individual preferences; a meditation practice outside, a vow of ahimsa – to do no avoidable harm – a commitment to vegetarianism or ethical consumerism, to give some examples. In this way our spirituality as neopagans is not separate from the rest of our lives but infuses and contains all aspects of it. We may be inspired to engage with both the healing of ourselves and our natural processes and systems, knowing that we are not independent of these, but interdependent. Many pagans get involved with climate change awareness groups such as Extinction Rebellion or Just Stop Oil, or with rewilding or reforestation projects, whether local or global, such as the grassroots TreeSisters, which aims to empower communities across the globe and runs various reforestation campaigns from Britain to the Amazon. If we are educators or therapists, we may explore practices based on these principles such as Forest School, or ecotherapy. There are myriad ways to connect our spirituality to our lives.

A place to begin, if you have not done so already, is to connect with the spirits of your own local land, whether your garden or a nearby forest, lake or park. You may like to try the following meditation.

Find a natural space that feels significant, vibrant, or simply peaceful to you. It could be a place you're already drawn to, like a favorite tree, a serene spot by a river, or a panoramic viewpoint.

Select a time when you are unlikely to be disturbed. Dawn or dusk are particularly potent times as they are transitional moments when the 'veil between worlds' is thin. Consider bringing an offering for the spirit of place. This should be something biodegradable and non-harmful to the environment such as seeds, water, or a small piece of food.

As you arrive at your chosen location, take some time to acclimate to the space. Walk around, breathe deeply, and allow your body to relax. Stand or sit comfortably, close your eyes, and imagine roots growing from the base of your spine or feet, going deep into the earth, anchoring you to this spot. Bring your awareness to your center, perhaps in your heart or solar plexus. Feel your energy collecting there, calming and centering your mind and body. Open your senses one by one. Note the smells, sounds, the feel of the air on your skin, and the taste of the place. Be present.

Inwardly or softly out loud, call to the spirit of the place. You might say something like:

> *"I call to the spirit of this place, the essence of the land. I come with respect and seek connection. I am here to listen and learn."*

Sit in silence, allowing the presence of the place to permeate your awareness. Notice any changes in your thoughts or feelings, any messages that may arise.

When it feels right to you, present your offering to the place with gratitude. This can be done simply by placing it on the ground, or you may wish to say something as you do so. Continue to meditate in the space, simply being present and open to the experience. Allow any insights or energies to flow through you. As you conclude your meditation, thank your surroundings and the spirit of place for what they have shared with you. Gently bring your awareness back to your physical self. Feel the ground beneath you, take a few deep breaths, and when you're ready, open your eyes.

After meditation, it can be beneficial to journal your experiences. Note any particular sensations, thoughts, or feelings that stood out to you. Consider visiting the same spot regularly to deepen the connection and observe the changes that come with different times and seasons. Connecting with the spirit of place is about cultivating a relationship. Like any relationship, it can deepen over time with respect, attention, and openness. This can also involve getting to know the history and stories of your place, and the local flora and fauna. What species of tree and shrub grow in abundance there? What and where is the oldest tree? What wildlife can you expect to see? Even a concrete jungle will have an abundance of wildlife and plantlife if you look for it, from birds to wily foxes to weeds pushing up through the cracks in the pavement. In fact, those very weeds, if you take the time to identify them, might turn out to be useful plants for your practice, whether medicinally or magically. And everywhere has a history. Talk to elderly locals, or teenagers, to find out local urban legends, and a trip to the local library should help you find anything newsworthy in the recent past as well as local folklore. It is always interesting – and often surprising – to find out if past folklore and modern urban legends have any shared themes. Or you could look even further into the past. What did your local area look like in the Middle Ages? The Iron Age? If you live in Britain or Ireland it was likely covered in ancient forest. Do any of the same tree species remain? An Internet search will also tell you which Celtic tribe lived in your area and what we know about them, and even what gods they worshiped. I was fascinated to find, for example, that where I live in the West Midlands was part of the area ruled by the Dobunni tribe. The Dobunni seem to have had the horse as a tribal totem and it has been suggested they worshiped a horse goddess; as they were pushed into South Wales after the invasion of the Saxons, and most of our references to the later Rhiannon are from the South of Wales, it may have been the Dobunni who brought her with them. (Morus-Baird, 2019) In a further link, Coventry, a small city in the West Midlands, is home to the famous legend of Lady Godiva, who allegedly rode around naked on a white horse…in May. You really might be surprised by what you discover when you start digging.

A word on the sense of place as sacred, however. Sense of place can all too often, when combined with an interest in ancestral lineage, in the wrong hands become a dark kind of nationalism and result in hostility to those from other places with different ancestral or national roots. This is where a pantheistic Goddess reminds us that we are all interrelated, all interconnected, often on a very practical level. Few of us, particularly in the West and particularly in Britain, can lay claim to a singular heritage or piece of land. We are all part of a complex and multi-layered web, and the part of it on which we stand is at once intimately sacred to us and yet indivisible from any other. This is an honoring of roots and land that echoes indigenous peoples all over the world far more than the nationalist sensibilities of a patriarchal far right. While this kind of thing is still mercifully rare in neopaganism, there are reports that it is on the rise, and so it's important to be on the watch for it if joining new groups with an intense focus on place or lineage or both.

Another way to give back to the Earth, whether locally or in widening circles, is to ask the question that Perceval missed; 'What ails thee?' What are the particular ecological problems in your place, your country, your continent? What problems are our place, if we are in the western world, contributing to? On a local level, we can help to support the rewilding of local areas, or the reintroduction of native species. If big projects are difficult due to accessibility, we can donate if we can afford to, or think smaller; a wildflower patch in our garden will attract pollinators and is an easy way to start rewilding, for example. If you are able to, you could switch to a renewable energy supplier.

Individual actions like these may not be a magical wand that will bring the change we need – huge systemic upheaval is needed for that – but it is a beginning, and a way to live our practice and our values, as well as bringing the energies of Modron deeper into our lives. A meaningful, and, I find, beautiful, way of working with her as a guardian goddess of the land is to make a pledge to commit to one action that can benefit your local or wider ecology. Make the pledge out loud, to Modron herself, perhaps at your altar and as part of a ritual. In the final chapter, I will offer suggestions to pledging yourself to her and invoking her support.

Chapter 8

Dedication to Modron

In neopagan practice, many individuals choose to work with a specific deity, either temporarily or for the long term, in order to foster a closer spiritual connection, gain insight, and enhance their personal growth. The god/dess one chooses often reflects qualities the individual wishes to draw into their life, or they may feel a particular call or affinity towards a certain deity. This process often involves dedicating oneself to the chosen deity for a set period, traditionally a year and a day. This time frame allows for a full cycle of seasonal energies and gives the practitioner ample time to deeply understand and connect with the deity's aspects and lessons. If you feel drawn to Modron, as I have written about here, and wish to understand her on a deeper level, consider dedicating yourself to her for a chosen period of time. This dedication does not mean exclusive worship; rather, it's an intensive focus on understanding and aligning with her attributes, teachings, and energies

Working with a personal goddess means integrating her stories, virtues, and symbols into one's life. This dedication is a profound commitment and should be entered into with seriousness and an open heart, ready for the transformative journey ahead. Consider setting up an altar dedicated to Modron, include her in daily prayers or meditations, celebrate her on relevant festival days, and conduct rituals in her name.

What follows is a suggestion for a dedication ritual to Modron, and a suggested invocation poem. As with all ritual suggestions in this book, take what you like, change what you don't.

Set up an altar, possibly facing the west, the direction associated with water and the setting sun. Place on it symbols of Modron/Matrona, such as images or statues, cups or cauldrons, river stones, and harvest grains or fruits. Include candles, perhaps in silver or blue, to represent the divine feminine and water

Choose a time when you can be undisturbed, ideally during twilight to reflect her connection to liminal spaces. Have a personal item that you wish to dedicate to Modron/Matrona, such as a piece of jewelry or a ritual tool.

Begin by purifying yourself and the space through your preferred method (e.g., smudging with sage, sprinkling salted water, or using sounds like a bell or chanting). Spend a few moments grounding yourself. Visualize roots growing from your feet into the earth, anchoring you firmly to the ground.

Call upon Modron/Matrona with an invocation poem such as the one below, or with your own heartfelt words, inviting her presence and blessing. Clearly state your intention to dedicate yourself to her for a year and a day. Speak from the heart, perhaps like so:

Great Mother Modron, I come before you to dedicate myself to your wisdom and path. For a year and a day, I seek to learn from your mysteries and to walk in your ways, so that I may grow in strength, compassion, and insight.

Present any offerings you have brought for Modron, such as food, drink, or crafts. Place them on the altar. Hold the item you are dedicating to Modron/Matrona in your hands, and ask for her blessing upon it. You might say:

Bless this [item], that it may be a bond between your divine essence and my mortal spirit.

Make a personal vow stating what you hope to achieve during this time and how you plan to work with Modron in your daily life. You may want to write it down in a journal or on a piece of parchment. Spend some time in quiet meditation, reflecting on Modron's role in your life and listening for any insights or messages. When you are ready, thank Modron for her presence and any insights provided.

Close the circle if you have cast one, and blow out the candles, saying:

> *Though the light is dimmed, the connection remains. May my dedication be as strong as the flame.*

Conclude your ritual with a simple feast to ground yourself. Eat and drink mindfully, seeing the food and water as gifts from the goddess.

Invocation to Modron

Oh Modron, Matrona, Great Mother divine,
Whose roots delve deep, where dark and light entwine,
From verdant grove to river's serpentine,
We call to thee, through whispered flower and vine
Hail, Goddess, from the cauldron's deep abyss,
Your wisdom sown in every season's kiss.
In autumn's gold and winter's cold remiss,
Your presence felt in spring's returning bliss
Beneath the moon's soft gaze, we seek your grace,
Your mantle of the starry cloak's embrace.
Oh Sovereign Queen of both time and space,
We seek the solace of your nurturing face
In you, the land and sky and sea do merge,
A sanctuary where troubled souls can purge
The heavy chains of life's relentless surge;

To your sacred shores, our weary hearts we urge
From the highest bough to the deepest sea,
Your essence permeates all, wild and free.
Great Matrona, in your sacred cup we find,
The elixir of peace for humankind.
As rivers to the vast ocean are led,
Guide our spirits, where no words are said.
Your hand in ours, forward we shall tread,
By your eternal wisdom ever fed
Ancient one, your name is sacred song,
Through the ages passed along.
Modron, Matrona, to you we belong,
In your embrace, reborn and strong
By leaf and by water, by stone and by bone,
I invoke you to make your presence known.
Goddess of life's tapestry, intricately sewn,
Upon this sacred altar, may your power be shown
As the river meets the sea, as the seed becomes the tree,
Merge your essence with my plea,
Modron, Matrona, I call to thee

Afterword

I hope that I have illustrated in this short book how Modron can be a powerful deity for those who wish to connect with her aspects of motherhood, healing and Sovereignty and how these still have wide-ranging relevance for spiritual seekers today. However, I also think that there may be much more to learn and discover about the Celtic Great Mother, and that she has further lessons to teach us, and significance and meaning to offer, providing her mythology is allowed to adapt and evolve. The Celtic stories were originally told orally, and while retaining core meaning they would have evolved with each telling. Stories that cannot change can only stagnate.

At the same time, we need to be able to dig back into the past for the bones of the more ancient stories, those which came before conquering heroes and initiating goddesses. In the standard Sovereignty tale, for example, the goddess or magical woman does little more than legitimize the hero-king, who is on the archetypal Hero's Journey, and possibly bear him children. Is this the version of her myth we need today, when arguably the archetypal masculine Hero's Journey has fed our modern myth of progress, leading to the colonization and neo-liberal economics that have helped fuel the climate crisis?

We cannot restore the Wasteland using the same stories which created it in the first place. Neither can we expect Matrona to keep pouring out her cornucopias if we are to continue misusing the Earth's resources. Perhaps we can turn to that story in the Elucidation, and to the all-important question that would restore the wounded king – what ails thee? For it will be compassion and community that gets us out of this mess, not conquest.

Modron's son, after all, is not Arthur, the warrior king. It is Mabon, the divine, magical child. The hunter who understands the beasts. The shaman. The bard who has drunk the Awen. Figures who symbolize the wild and our living, breathing connection with it. Figures who remember the stories that we need most of all, right now.

We must all be the Mother now, giving birth to the Divine Child, the light, within ourselves. Bring this light back out from imprisonment and exile. No conquering solitary hero is coming to save us. The Second Coming is not, in fact, coming. Arthur is not going to turn up with Excalibur. But we do have each other, and we may be able, if we work together, to save ourselves.

We are the Mabon.

Note to Readers

Thank you for purchasing *Modron; Meeting the Celtic Mother Goddess.* I sincerely hope that you got as much from reading this book as I did from writing it, and that it whets your appetite for finding out more about these topics. If you have a few moments, I would be grateful if you could leave a review at your preferred online site. Also, if you would like to connect with me, read my blog, or find out more about forthcoming titles, please visit my website at kellebandea.wixsite.com or follow me on Twitter @DeaKelle.

Bright blessings
Kelle BanDea

References

Baring-Gould, Sabine. *Lives of the Saints* (1898) reprinted 2009 by Cornell University Library

Beck, Noemie. *The River Goddess in Celtic Traditions; Mother, Healer and Wisdom Purveyor* (2015) Melannges en l'honneur de Pierre Yves-Lambert hal-03275671

Blackie, Sharon. *If Women Rose Rooted* (2016) September Publishing

Bottrell, William. *Traditions and Hearthside Stories of West Cornwall vol 2* (1873)

https://sacred-texts.com/neu/celt/swc2/swc253.htm accessed 27/10/23

Bromwich, Rachel. ed. *Trioedd Ynys Prydein: The Triads of the Island of Britain* (2006) University of Wales Press

Coulson, S, Segadika, P, Walker, N. *Ritual in the Hunter-Gatherer/ Early Pastoralist Period; Evidence from Tsodilo Hills, Botswana* (2016) African Archaeological Review 33 pp205-222

Dashu, Max. *Witches and Pagans; Women in European Folk Tradition 700-1100 (Secret History of the Witches 7)* (2017) Veleda Press

De Troyes, Chretien. *Perceval* (1190) in *Arthurian Romances* (1991) Penguin Classics

Gildas, St. *On the Ruin of Britain* (550 AD) reprinted 2009 by Serenity Publishers, LLC

Gruffydd, William John. *Rhiannon; An Inquiry into the Origin of the First and Third Branches of the Mabinogi* (1881) reprinted 2021 Hassel St Press

Hughes, Kristoffer. *Celtic Magic* (2013) Llewellyn Books

Jones, Kathy. (2021) https://kathyjones.co.uk/ accessed 31/10/23

Koch, John T. *Celtic Culture; A Historical Encyclopaedia* (2005) ABC-CLIO

Lacy, Norris J. *The Spoils of Annwfn* in *The New Arthurian Encyclopedia,* (1991) Garland

Lewis, Gwyneth and William, Rowan. (trans) *The Book of Taliesin; Poems of Warfare and Praise in an Enchanted Britain* (2019) Penguin

Matthews, Caitlin. *Mabon and the Guardians of Celtic Britain; Hero Myths in the Mabinogion* (2002) Inner Traditions

Monmouth, Geoffrey of. *Vita Merlini* (1150) reprinted 2011 Amberley Publishing

Morus-Baird, Gwilym. *Is Rhiannon a Goddess?* (2019) Celtic Source; Exploring the Myths of the Celtic Nations https://celticsource.online/celtic-source-is-rhiannon-a-goddess/ accessed 6/11/2023

Paice MacLeod, Sharon. *Celtic Cosmology and the Otherworld; Mythic Origins, Sovereignty and Liminality* (2018) MacFarland Publishing

Telyndru, Jhenah. *Avalon Within: A Sacred Journey of Myth, Mystery and Inner Wisdom* (2010) Llewellyn Books

Thompson, Albert Wilder. ed. *The Elucidation; a prologue to the Conte du Graal* (1931) Publications of the institute of French Studies

Von Zatzikhoven, Ulrich. *Lanzelet* (1191) in *Arthurian Studies* (2000) D.S. Brewer

Witzel, E.J. Michael. *The Origins of the World's Mythologies* (2013) Oxford University Press

For my favorite translation of the *Mabinogi* see Sioned Davies *The Mabinogion* published 2007 by Oxford World Classics.

The *Welsh Triads* and MS Peniarth 147 can be found online at the National Library of Wales https://www.library.wales/ I also recommend Rachel Bromwich's treatment of the *Triads*, listed above.

Genealogy of the Saints can be found in The Cambro-Briton (1821) Vol3 Number 23

available at https://www.jstor.org/stable/30069154 accessed 2/11/2023

MOON BOOKS

PAGANISM & SHAMANISM

What is Paganism? A religion, a spirituality, an alternative belief system, nature worship? You can find support for all these definitions (and many more) in dictionaries, encyclopedias, and text books of religion, but subscribe to any one and the truth will evade you. Above all Paganism is a creative pursuit, an encounter with reality, an exploration of meaning and an expression of the soul. Druids, Heathens, Wiccans and others, all contribute their insights and literary riches to the Pagan tradition. Moon Books invites you to begin or to deepen your own encounter, right here, right now.

If you have enjoyed this book, why not tell other readers by posting a review on your preferred book site.

Bestsellers from Moon Books
Pagan Portals Series

The Morrigan

Meeting the Great Queens

Morgan Daimler

Ancient and enigmatic, the Morrigan reaches out to us. On shadowed wings and in raven's call, meet the ancient Irish goddess of war, battle, prophecy, death, sovereignty, and magic.

Paperback: 978-1-78279-833-0 ebook: 978-1-78279-834-7

The Awen Alone

Walking the Path of the Solitary Druid

Joanna van der Hoeven

An introductory guide for the solitary Druid, The Awen Alone will accompany you as you explore, and seek out your own place within the natural world.

Paperback: 978-1-78279-547-6 ebook: 978-1-78279-546-9

Moon Magic

Rachel Patterson

An introduction to working with the phases of the Moon, what they are and how to live in harmony with the lunar year and to utilise all the magical powers it provides.

Paperback: 978-1-78279-281-9 ebook: 978-1-78279-282-6

Hekate

A Devotional

Vivienne Moss

Hekate, Queen of Witches and the Shadow-Lands, haunts the pages of this devotional bringing magic and enchantment into your lives.

Paperback: 978-1-78535-161-7 ebook: 978-1-78535-162-4

Bestsellers from Moon Books

Keeping Her Keys

An Introduction to Hekate's Modern Witchcraft

Cyndi Brannen

Blending Hekate, witchcraft and personal development together to create a powerful new magickal perspective.

Paperback: 978-1-78904-075-3 ebook 978-1-78904-076-0

Journey to the Dark Goddess

How to Return to Your Soul

Jane Meredith

Discover the powerful secrets of the Dark Goddess and transform your depression, grief and pain into healing and integration.

Paperback: 978-1-84694-677-6 ebook: 978-1-78099-223-5

Shamanic Reiki

Expanded Ways of Working with Universal Life Force Energy

Llyn Roberts, Robert Levy

Shamanism and Reiki are each powerful ways of healing; together, their power multiplies. Shamanic Reiki introduces techniques to help healers and Reiki practitioners tap ancient healing wisdom.

Paperback: 978-1-84694-037-8 ebook: 978-1-84694-650-9

Southern Cunning

Folkloric Witchcraft in the American South

Aaron Oberon

Modern witchcraft with a Southern flair, this book is a journey through the folklore of the American South and a look at the power these stories hold for modern witches.

Paperback: 978-1-78904-196-5 ebook: 978-1-78904-197-2